To

The dark blue ghosts of Portishead, 1944

Fire and the Law

Fire and the Law

an

introductory guide to the
Law relating to Fire

by

ANN R. EVERTON, LL.M., Ph.D.,

of Lincoln's Inn, Barrister
Lecturer in Law at the University of Leicester

LONDON

BUTTERWORTHS

1972

ENGLAND: BUTTERWORTH & CO. (PUBLISHERS) LTD.
                LONDON · 88 KINGSWAY, WC2B 6AB

AUSTRALIA: BUTTERWORTH & CO. (AUSTRALIA) LTD.
                SYDNEY: 586 PACIFIC HIGHWAY, CHATSWOOD, NSW 2067
                MELBOURNE: 343 LITTLE COLLINS STREET, 3000
                BRISBANE: 240 QUEEN STREET, 4000

CANADA: BUTTERWORTH & CO. (CANADA) LTD.
                TORONTO: 14 CURITY AVENUE, 374

NEW ZEALAND: BUTTERWORTH & CO. (NEW ZEALAND) LTD.
                WELLINGTON: 26-28 WARING TAYLOR STREET, 1

SOUTH AFRICA: BUTTERWORTH & CO. (SOUTH AFRICA) (PTY.) LTD.
                DURBAN: 152-154 GALE STREET

ISBN 0 406 57740 4

Printed by Eyre & Spottiswoode Ltd., Thanet Press, Margate

PREFACE

This little book owes its origin to a request made by an Officer of the City of Birmingham Fire Brigade. On the face of it, it was a straightforward request: "Write a book on the law relating to fire." At once, however, he proceeded to attach to it stringent conditions. "Make it *simple*," he urged me. "Keep out the 'therefores,' the 'wherefores' and the 'heretofores.' Keep it clear and to the point. People who are concerned with fire protection are fundamentally practical people: write it so *they would want to read it*."

The pages which follow contain my attempt to fulfil his requirements; but at the outset I must emphasize that the law relating to fire is a very large and intricate subject, and that to write upon it in detail would result in a book many times the size of this one. That which follows, however, is essentially an introduction to the subject, a simple outline of its principal features.

In writing such a guide my aim has been primarily to assist those members of the Fire Service who, as they climb the ladder of promotion, are called upon to make a study of the law relating to fire; but I have borne in mind also that this is a subject of interest to all those people who are concerned with the protection of life and property from damage done by fire. Whatever the sphere of my reader's calling then, I hope he will find the ensuing pages of interest and value. If no more, perhaps it will enable him to 'see the wood for the trees'.

To conclude, a few words of thanks are appropriate. To Butterworths I owe my gratitude for their continued kindness and assistance; to Miss Bayliss for her ability to convert my unintelligible scrawl into a beautifully typed script; and to my family for their patience and encouragement. And finally, to many

Officers of the Fire Service I owe my gratitude for their interest, courtesy and generous hospitality. They will perhaps gather the measure of my appreciation when they find I have dedicated my effort to certain of their predecessors, namely, to a small group of firemen who belonged to the Service in the dark days of the early 'forties, when England underwent her ordeal by fire.

20th March, 1972   A.R.E.

CONTENTS

PART ONE

Part 1 of this little book is intended purely for those who are studying the law relating to fire as an examination subject, and who have never had cause to study the English legal system. It is an attempt to provide, in as few pages as possible, general "background" information which will enable such students to place in its proper context the material which is contained in Part 11.

Chapter 1

ABOUT THE LAW

As a subject for study, the law presents two basic problems: on the one hand its *size*, and on the other hand its *detail*. Very soon, the law student learns that he has chosen a subject which is rather like a vast and intricate jigsaw puzzle . . .

Our interest lies, of course, in but one piece of that jigsaw puzzle, namely the law relating to fire, but before we can examine that particular piece we must first have some idea of the picture of which it forms a part. It would be possible, I suppose, to commit to memory some of the points on fire law and claim a nodding acquaintance with the topic, but a proper appreciation of it requires a sense of perspective, and that can be gained only by knowing something of the law as a whole.

First, then, we must consider the idea of "law", and, in particular, the system of law which governs us in this country.

(i) *The idea of "law"*

If you asked an average Englishman the question "what is law?" he would "um" and "ah" as he groped for an answer: but if you asked that same individual whether he had heard phrases such as, "I'll have the law on you . . .", or "it's the long arm of the law . . ." or "there goes Johnny Law . . .", he would most likely say "yes, many times". Now, if he thought about these phrases for a minute, he would find that they told him more than a little about the law. In the first phrase he would see reflected the *protection* which the law affords him, in the second, the *punishment* which infraction of it invites, and in the third, the need for its day-to-day enforcement. In fact, three of the principal features of law emerge from those most common phrases. Yet those phrases only tell one something about the law; they do not tell one what law *is* . . .

For a very long time, those interested in "Jurisprudence" (i.e., the science of law), have tried to provide a satisfactory definition of law, but it has proved a hopeless task. For our purpose, though, it will suffice if we content ourselves with a simple explanation. Very simply, law is a collection of rules which, over centuries, members of society develop for the governing of their activities, their relationship with each other, and their dealing with property. They are rules which are slowly established to replace "force" as a means of resolving disputes, and they are rules which are obeyed because society imposes sanctions for disobedience. Moreover, as between one society and another systems of law differ, for each society evolves a system of law which suits its own particular requirements. Again, notice that I say *"evolves"*: this is important. Always one must remember that a system of law is a living, growing thing, capable of adapting itself to meet the ever-changing needs of the society to which it belongs. In short, it never stands still.

So much then for the idea of "law" in general: now we must narrow the field of vision and confine our attention to the system of law which prevails in England.

(ii) *Law in England*

(a) The scope of English law

In order to acquire an idea of the *scope* of English law one should go into a large, technical bookshop and browse amongst the shelves devoted to law books. A short while scanning the titles will indicate clearly the width and diversity of English law. On the one hand there will be seen books on those branches of the law which lawyers call "public law", so called because they involve the relationship of the State and the individual. These books will be on such topics as the law relating to government, to tax, to crime, and to social services. On the other hand, there will be seen books on those branches of the law which lawyers call "private law", so called because they involve the relationship of private individuals, one with the other. These books will include such topics as the law of contract,[1] the law of tort,[2] the law of property and family law. In both categories, though, will be found also highly specialised books, such as, for instance, those on the law relating to town and country planning, to companies, to patents, to factories, or to restrictive trade practices . . .

To the non-lawyer all these titles present a bewildering and formidable array. Having looked through them, one may privately agree with the layman who could not believe there were so many *sorts* of law! On a more serious note, though, a few minutes spent amongst legal text books is an ideal way of gaining a bird's eye view of the expansive field covered by our modern legal system. But that is as far as it goes. If one wants to know about the law itself, one has to be prepared for a little history. Inasmuch as the law is a living, growing body of rules, an understanding of it leads inevitably to two questions, how has it grown and what are its sources?

(b) The sources and growth of English law

To trace the growth of English law is to see unfolded a story which has lasted without interruption for nearly a thousand years, and which proceeds even as one writes. Our law, it has been said, is like a river which flows continuously, a river moreover, which flows from three main sources. These sources are known to lawyers as (1) the common law; (2) equity; and (3) legislation. Let us then take a look at each of them in turn:

(1) *The common law.* In the days before the Norman Conquest, England had no system of law which was common to the country

---

[1]By the law of contract is meant the law which governs commercial agreements, whether those agreements are of the most simple or the most complicated kind.
[2]By the law of tort is meant the law which governs private injuries. If, in one or more of a number of ways, X injures Y or Y's property, (perhaps by slandering him or trespassing on his land), X is said to have committed a "tort", and Y can seek compensation from him. This he does by "suing X for damages".

as a whole. At that time England was composed of numerous isolated communities, each being governed by its own customary rules of behaviour. Under Norman rule, however, the multi-coloured threads of local customs were slowly woven by the royal judges into a system of law which was common throughout the land. The significance of this development can hardly be overstated, for the "common law" as it became known has remained from mediaeval times to the present day the very heart of our legal system.

That it should have done so is a remarkable feat: and it is not surprising that lawyers the world over express deep admiration for the English common law. It owes its unusual success to its essentially *practical* character, and its character it owes in turn to its composition. Very simply, it is an accumulation of judges' decisions, an accumulation which has been building up day by day for centuries. Every time a case is taken to an important court, the decision which the judge reaches, or to be more accurate, *the reason on which he bases his decision*, becomes an integral part of the common law. Thus, you see, the common law stems from the actual answers given to actual questions, and this means that the legal principles which gradually emerge from the judges' decisions do not emerge as "airy-fairy" abstract policies, but as solid, down to earth rules, forged, as it has been said, on the "anvil of reality". To its essentially practical character, moreover, must be added one further quality which is of equally vital significance, namely, its *coherence*. The common law is not a vast, jumbled-up heap of decisions, it is an orderly body of law. That this is so is due to the attitude of judges: they have always taken the view that cases of a similar nature should be decided in a similar fashion, for that is the only way to consistency and certainty. Thus, whenever a judge is called upon to reach a decision, he searches through the decisions given in preceding cases of a like nature to the one in front of him, and then, in making his own decision, he follows those which have gone before. This idea of following past decisions is known as the doctrine of "judicial precedent", and it is this doctrine which makes the law certain, consistent and coherent. Indeed, one could say that the doctrine of judicial precedent is the cement which binds together the bricks of the common law.

(2) *Equity*. As the second of our three sources of law we have to consider "equity". Now equity is a body of law which owes its origin to the teething troubles of the infant common law.

Legal historians tell us that it is usual for legal systems in their infancy to go through a period of excessive formality and technicality, a period when the nascent rules of law are unduly rigid, and still lacking in the maturity which will one day make them flexible. When this was the unhappy state of the common law, those whom it denied justice sent humble petitions for assistance to the King. In the course of time these petitions became so numerous that the task of their adjudication was delegated to the chancellor, and it was from the decisions given by successive chancellors that there developed the body of law known as equity. Unlike the royal judges who administered the common law, the chancellors were not bound by strict, technical rules, and, being men of the Church, they decided the cases which came before them in accordance with the dictates of *conscience*. Thus, equity was built up on the simple but fundamental concepts of moral duty, honour and integrity, the very word "equity" signifying "fairness".

On the face of it, it might seem odd that two bodies of law could grow up side by side, the common law in the common law courts, and equity in the chancellors' "Court of Chancery". That they could flourish in this way is due to the fact that they were not rival systems of law, but complementary systems. Indeed, the chancellors were careful not to contradict the rules of common law, for their object was to fashion rules which would carry on where the rules of common law left off. Equity, you see, was designed to fill in the gaps left by the common law, to *supplement* it, or, in the words of a famous lawyer, to be "a gloss" upon it. Of course, there was occasional friction, even hostility, but by and large the two systems developed harmoniously, it being established long ago that in the event of any *possible* conflict, equity should prevail.

The story of the contribution which equity has made to the development of English law is a long and interesting one. It so happens, however, that on certain branches of the law the principles of equity do not have great bearing, and such is the case with the law relating to fire. Accordingly, other than to

7

CHAPTER I—ABOUT THE LAW

note it as a source of law, and, in many fields a most significant source, we do not need to consider it further.

(3) *Legislation*. Now we must turn to the third source of our law, legislation.[3] This is the law which is made (or "enacted") by Parliament, and inasmuch as it emanates formally from the Sovereign, it is regarded as pre-eminent amongst the sources of law. There is, though, a fundamental difference between legislation as a source of law, and common law and equity as sources of law, for the rules of common law and equity, it will be recalled, emerge from series of judicial decisions. Those who fashion legislation are trying to lay down rules which will cover and provide for all sorts of future contingencies, but judges are concerned with the immediate resolution of the particular dispute before them, and it is only after numerous similar disputes have arisen, that principles of law begin to grow. Thus, legislation is a *direct* form of law making, while common law and equity are "judge made law", and so develop as an *indirect* form of law making.

When considering the idea of legislation, mention must be made also of what is called "delegated legislation". The pressures of modern life are such that Parliament often has to delegate to certain people and certain bodies the power to make laws. Parliament itself passes legislation[4] which provides a framework, and the less exalted make the laws which fill in the details; an arrangement the use of which is at present increasing to a remarkable extent.

In the study of the law relating to fire, one is concerned a great deal with the study of legislation and delegated legislation, so a little later there will be found a reference to a note on how to use and understand these particular forms of law making.

So then, there they are; common law, equity, and legislation; the three sources of the constantly flowing river which we call English law.

(c) The working of English law
When we speak of the working of English law we mean the

---

[3]Or, in other words, Acts of Parliament, or Statutes.
[4]The technical way of saying "makes an Act of Parliament".

8

way in which it is brought to bear upon everyday life, or, to put it more simply, the "machinery" of English law. This machinery is very large and complicated, and to appreciate it properly it is necessary to see it in motion, but for our purpose it will be sufficient to take a look at the principal features, namely, the courts, the procedure, and the personnel of the law.

(1) *The courts.* The first important thing to notice about our courts of law is that they are arranged in ladders, or, more precisely, in *hierarchies*, i.e., they ascend from the lowly to the exalted. This means that a person who is not satisfied with a decision reached in one court can, as it is said, "appeal" to a higher court and seek satisfaction there, a state of affairs which is of special significance in the context of "judicial precedent". From the explanation given earlier it will be recalled that judges are required to follow the decisions reached in former, similar cases. Now, though, one is in a position to appreciate a refinement to that rule, and in general terms it is this: Judges are obliged to follow the decisions reached in similar past cases in courts which are *superior* to the one in which they are sitting, but not those reached in courts which are *inferior*. Were it not so, the idea of "appealing" from one court to the next would not be worthwhile.

The next important point to notice about the courts concerns *"Jurisdiction"*, by which is meant the *sphere* in which a court has power to act. Here, what one needs to understand is the difference which exists between what is known as a "criminal jurisdiction" and a "civil jurisdiction". When one speaks of a court having a "criminal jurisdiction" one means that it is empowered to hear criminal cases, i.e., to try people who are alleged to have committed an offence. When, however, one speaks of a court having a "civil jurisdiction" one means it is empowered to hear civil cases, i.e., cases which are so called because they arise from citizens' private disputes.

This distinction between criminal and civil matters is fundamental, and vital to grasp. Criminal law, as has been seen, is a branch of *public* law: when a person commits a crime he offends society at large, and he is prosecuted on behalf of society. There is nothing public, though, about civil law, for "civil" is the

9

label which is placed on those branches of law which are concerned with purely private disputes and in which society at large has no interest, (including, for example, the law of torts and the law of contract). Thus, the very objects of criminal and civil law differ: whereas the former seeks to punish those who wrong the public, the latter seeks to resolve the citizens' personal disputes.[5]

Moreover, the difference is reflected in the fact that while basically the method of trial is the same, criminal and civil cases are conducted in somewhat different ways and according to different rules.

Once this important distinction is appreciated it becomes clear what is meant when it is said that in this country there are two ladders or hierarchies of courts. On the one hand there is a hierarchy of civil courts, and on the other hand a hierarchy of criminal courts. At the lower end of the ladder in each case one meets what are known as the courts of "first instance", i.e., the courts to which cases are first taken (in the criminal sphere the Magistrates' Courts, and in the civil sphere the County Courts or the High Court). Again, at the upper end of the ladder one meets in each case what are known as the courts of "appellate jurisdiction", i.e., the courts to which appeals are made. Thus, in criminal cases appeals may be made to the Criminal Division of the Court of Appeal, and in civil cases to the Civil Division of the Court of Appeal. Further, at the pinnacle of both hierarchies there is the House of Lords, the ultimate court of appeal in the land for criminal *and* civil cases. Thus, in technical language, it possesses both criminal and civil jurisdiction. If, however, one were to undertake a detailed study of the court system, one would find that the House of Lords is not unique in that particular respect, for at other points in the two ladders one meets courts which exercise jurisdiction over cases of each kind.

Next, let us consider the second aspect of the machinery of the law, namely, procedure:

(2) *Procedure.* When a case is brought before a court, the actual hearing of that case and the earlier events which culminate

---

[5]Such a personal dispute could arise for example if X breaks his contract with Y, or if X slanders Y, or again, if X trespasses on Y's land.

in its hearing are governed by certain rules. These rules are called "rules of procedure", or, more simply "procedure", and they are divided into two different groups: on the one hand there are the rules of civil procedure, and on the other hand there are the rules of criminal procedure.

The rules of procedure, both civil and criminal, are complicated, and form a subject for study in themselves; but their object is simple: they are designed to ensure that the parties involved in a case get a fair hearing, and that justice is done. This the reader may discover for himself if his duties as a fire officer take him into court, and he sees the rules of procedure in action. Actual contact, moreover, will convince him of the need to apply these rules with care and precision.

Finally, in this context, a distinction must be made between the words "procedure" and "proceedings", for the two are often confused. As we have just noted, the name "procedure" is given to two sets of rules. The name "proceedings" is given, however, not to *rules*, but to a series of *events*, namely the series of events which occurs when a case is heard.

Last, but by no means least, let us take a look at the personnel of the law.

(3) *Personnel.* While the machinery of justice involves the contribution of many different occupations, we will confine our attention to the three which appear in the forefront, namely, those of the solicitor, the barrister and the judge.

In this country, the legal profession is divided into two branches: solicitors and barristers; each branch of the profession carrying out different work, and being trained in rather different ways. It is a division, moreover, which is at the moment under considerable attack, and about which arguments can be raised both for and against.

The solicitor, of course, is the one who comes into direct contact with the public. He is essentially a businessman, and generally, though not essentially, his sphere of activity is wider than that of the barrister. Of a country solicitor this is especially true, for within the space of a few days he may have to turn from the ins and outs of a car crash, to the intricacies of a conveyance of property, and then to the details of a divorce petition. It is his city counterpart who is more likely to find the conditions for specialisation in one or other branches of the law.

The solicitor must be contrasted with the barrister, whose work does not bring him into direct contact with the public, and who is indeed denied such contact. What then is the work of the barrister? In general terms he spends his days fighting cases in court, preparing accurately the manner in which such cases will be presented in court, and giving opinions on various points of law. It is in fact the barrister alone who has the right to appear in all the courts, the solicitor being allowed to appear only in the lower courts. Thus, if it is desired to fight a case in, say, the High Court, a barrister must be "briefed to appear". The solicitor will do all the preliminary work of gathering the relevant material, but it is up to the barrister to make the best use of that material in court.

In this country it is from the ranks of the highly experienced and successful lawyers[6] that the judges are drawn; a system which evokes surprised comments from lawyers who come from countries where it is believed that judges and advocates should be trained in different ways. Nevertheless, it is a system which for centuries has proved its worth. From what has been said about the development of common law and equity as "judge made" systems of law it will be appreciated that great importance is attached to the status of a judge. The decisions which a judge makes become part and parcel of the very fabric of our law, and it is essential that he be a lawyer of outstanding qualities. Again, it is equally essential for him to remain free and independent. No political or other outside influence should impair the free exercise of his duties. So long, indeed, as a judge of the High Court, the Court of Appeal or the House of Lords remains of good behaviour, it requires an address by both Houses of Parliament to remove him.

CONCLUSION

In the preceding few pages an attempt has been made to provide, as a background for the material which follows, a

---

[6]Often, but not invariably, from barristers who have achieved the standing of "Queen's Counsel".

bird's eye view of the idea of law, and more especially of law in England: its scope, its sources and its working. Of course, pressure of time and space has caused one to skim along the peaks of the subject, leaving in shadow the deep valleys which lie between. It is well known that to cram the proverbial quart into the proverbial pint pot leads to distortion, and here it is a matter of gallons rather than quarts! Even so, it is believed to be essential to grasp the fundamentals of a system before studying in detail any special or particular portion of it.

PART TWO

For those readers who have examinations ahead, and for whom the study of English law is, as yet, a novelty, a caution is in point. It was explained in Chapter 1 that the study of the law relating to fire frequently involves the consideration of legislation and delegated legislation. In the fourth appendix to this little book will be found a note on how to use and understand these forms of law making, and it is earnestly suggested that this be read next.

Chapter 2

THE ORGANISATION OF THE FIRE SERVICE

INTRODUCTION

In dealing with the organisation of the fire service, one has to take in a number of matters: the structure of the service, the duties and powers of fire authorities, the establishment and running of fire brigades, the special powers given by Parliament to firemen, and (last but not least), the supply of water. This is a sizeable field to cover, but it will assist if it is explained at the outset that, generally speaking, we can look for the basic law on these matters in one place, namely the Fire Services Act 1947.[1] In this chapter frequent reference will be made to that Act, so it will be called simply the "1947 Act".

Let us then consider in turn the various matters which have been listed above, and so try to build up a sketch of the legal organisation of the fire fighting service in this country.

A. THE STRUCTURE OF THE SERVICE

If we seek the actual structure or "set up" of the service, we must begin by looking in ss. 1 and 4 of the 1947 Act. From s. 4 we gather that County and County Borough Councils are made the "fire authority" for the area of the council, and from s. 1(1) we learn that every fire authority is under a duty to make

---

[1] It should be noticed that in certain places this Act has been amended by the Fire Services Act 1959, but this will be taken into account in the explanation which is given.

17

provision for fire fighting purposes.[2] In particular, s. 1(1) goes on to say that every fire authority must make sure it secures for its area the efficient services of a fire brigade.[3] So it comes to this: The Act makes the larger councils the "fire authority" for the area covered by the council, and fire authorities must make provision for fire fighting purposes by seeing that they secure (amongst other things), the efficient services of a fire brigade. Thus it is a simple enough basis.

Reading further, we find that the 1947 Act provides for what is known as a "combined fire authority". Such authorities are set up by what are known as "combination schemes", under which two or more fire authorities are combined for fire fighting purposes. (The reason for doing it is clear: expediency).

If we look in s. 5 of the Act we shall see that such schemes can be entered into by fire authorities voluntarily, and that the schemes will operate if they are approved by the Secretary of State. On the other hand, though, we shall find if we look at s. 6 that the Secretary is given the power to initiate such a scheme himself, if he considers it expedient in the interests of efficiency.

The combination schemes must provide, amongst other matters, for the constitution of a fire authority for the combined area, and for the establishment of a fire brigade for that area. And, of course, it is only fair that the combined fire authority should consist of representatives from each of the areas involved in the scheme.

Continuing still further with the story, there is the chance that fire authorities may need or wish to collaborate with others to a certain extent, but not to the extreme extent of actual combination. The need for, or the possibility of, such collaboration is met in ss. 2 and 12 of the 1947 Act, s. 2 providing for what are called "reinforcement schemes" and s. 12 providing for what are called "agency arrangements".

Let us look first at "reinforcement schemes", the idea of which is the provision of mutual assistance.

Section 2 places a duty on fire authorities to join in the making of reinforcement schemes to secure the rendering of mutual

---

[2] By "fire fighting purposes" are meant the extinction of fires, and the protection of life and property from fire.
[3] See s.1(1)(a).

assistance with fires occurring in each other's area. It is a duty
which is imposed "so far as is practicable", and a duty which
arises only in certain circumstances, viz:
> *either* where it is necessary to supplement the services provided
> by the fire authority in whose area fire breaks out;
> *or* where reinforcement at any time can be more readily
> obtained from the resources of other fire authorities than
> from the one in whose area fire occurs.[4]

Moreover, s. 2 not only puts on the fire authority this duty[5]
to join in such a scheme, but also a duty to carry the scheme into
effect.

Any reinforcement scheme so made must be notified to the
Secretary of State, and in certain circumstances the Secretary
himself may make one.

Finally, in this context it should be noticed that provision is
also made for the operation of a reinforcement scheme with the
owners of a private fire brigade (such as is kept, for example,
by large industrial concerns). If a fire authority makes such a
scheme with a private brigade, then of course terms may be
arranged as to payment or otherwise.

Now, then, let us turn from reinforcement schemes to "agency
arrangements".

Section 12 explains that a fire authority is able to discharge
its functions by making arrangements for either another fire
authority or the owners of a private fire brigade to act as its
agent; and again, that the Secretary can himself initiate such an
arrangement if he thinks it expedient. Furthermore, the fire
authority is able to make the arrangement apply to all or any
part of its area, and, where relevant, terms as to payment or
otherwise can be agreed.

Before leaving ss. 2 and 12, there remains one important point to
be noticed. Section 2 places a DUTY on fire authorities, so far as is
practicable and where certain situations exist, to join in the making
of a reinforcement scheme. There is obligation because there is
need. Section 12, however, is not couched in terms of *obligation*, it

---

[4] In the first case it is a matter of the authority's provision being inadequate,
and in the second case it is a matter of geography.
[5] It is important to remember always the limits of the duty.

merely says what a fire authority *can* do. Here, there is nothing about a *duty*, for the context is different.

From what has been said about fire authorities, it will have become apparent that the "set up" is not necessarily as simple as ss. 1 and 4 would suggest. There is always the likelihood that the service is provided by a combined fire authority, or by resort to reinforcement schemes or agency arrangements. Yet all the possible variations have a common basis, and it is *the promotion of efficiency*. Indeed, the idea of an *efficient* service runs through the Act like a golden thread: one meets it time and time again . . .

(It will have been noticed that in explaining these matters there has been need on a number of occasions to refer to the Secretary of State, and in the next few pages there will be found still further references to that office. The old and highly important office of Secretary of State is one through which communication can be made between the Sovereign and the individual. Although the office itself is *one*,[6] the duties of the office are divided between a number of persons, and one finds, for example, such persons as the Home Secretary and the Secretary for Defence, featuring amongst them. The task of administering the 1947 Act was entrusted to the Secretary of State, and it is the Home Secretary who acquired the task. So, when reference is made to the Secretary of State, one means in fact the Home Secretary. He it is who carries the responsibility for the provision of the service; he it is who sits at the apex of the structure).[7]

B. THE DUTIES AND POWERS OF FIRE AUTHORITIES

To understand the fundamental duties cast upon fire authorities it is necessary to proceed in detail through the provisions of s.1(1) of the 1947 Act; a subsection of the Act on which we have already touched.

Section 1(1), it may be recalled, places a duty on every fire authority to make provision for fire fighting purposes. Having established this general duty, the same subsection then adds:

---

[6]A hovering, ghost-like entity!
[7]To advise him, though, on fire service matters there is a body called the Central Fire Brigades Advisory Council. Again, notice further that while in England the Home Secretary administers the Act, in Scotland the task is undertaken by the Secretary of State for Scotland.

"and in particular, every fire authority shall secure:

(a) the services for their area of such a fire brigade and such equipment as may be necessary to meet efficiently all normal requirements;[8]

(b) the efficient training of the members of the fire brigade;

(c) efficient arrangements for dealing with calls for the assistance of the fire brigade in case of fire and for summoning members of the fire brigade;

(d) efficient arrangements for obtaining, by inspection or otherwise, information required for fire fighting purposes with respect to the character of the buildings and other property in the area of the fire authority, the available water supplies and the means of access thereto, and other material local circumstances;

(e) efficient arrangements for ensuring that reasonable steps are taken to prevent or mitigate damage to property resulting from measures taken in dealing with fires;

(f) efficient arrangements for the giving, when requested, of advice in respect of buildings and other property in the area of the fire authority as to fire prevention, restricting the spread of fires, and means of escape in case of fire."

All in all, therefore, a great deal is required of a fire authority. The requirements seem, though, reasonably clear, and to sum them up briefly it may be said that a fire authority must secure a brigade, equipment, training facilities, and arrangements for dealing with calls, for obtaining necessary information, for minimising damage and for giving advice on fire precautions.

While the paragraphs are all easy to follow, however, and do not require further explanation, one or two comments must be made before continuing further:

First, in connection with para. (d),[9] it is necessary to read also s. 1(2) of the Act. Section 1(2) provides that for the purposes of s. 1(1)(d)[10] any member of a fire brigade maintained by a fire authority shall have a power to enter premises. To exercise such a

---

[8]We have already been obliged to touch on s.1(1)(a).

[9]Paragraph (d) is concerned with securing arrangements for obtaining necessary information.

[10]I.e., for the purpose of obtaining information.

power he needs written authority from his fire authority, and then he may enter at all reasonable hours.[11]

Secondly, it is of interest to contrast with para. (*d*) para. (*f*).[12] In para. (*d*), one notices, Parliament is concerned with the ability of a fire authority to *acquire* the information it needs, while in para. (*f*) it is concerned with the desirability of the fire authority *giving* advice. So paras. (*d*) and (*f*) proceed in opposite directions. Both paragraphs, it should be noted, are widely used and practised within the fire service. Obviously there is a constant need to obtain information, for fire-fighting purposes, regarding the nature of buildings and other property in the area of the fire authority; and, equally obviously, a constant desirability that advice be given, when requested, on fire prevention, the restriction of the spread of fire, and means of escape in the event of fire.

Finally, it is worthwhile noticing that the idea of efficiency appears in each and every one of the paragraphs (*a*) to (*f*); it is a constant reminder of the theme of the 1947 Act, and the grave nature of the public need which it seeks to fulfil.[13]

Turning then from the *duties* to the *powers* of a fire authority, let us consider s. 3(1) of the 1947 Act. It is from this subsection one gathers many of the powers of a fire authority, including power:

(*a*) to provide accommodation for the fire brigade and its equipment (including residential accommodation for members of the brigade);

(*b*) to pay people who render services for fire fighting purposes other than firemen;

(*c*) to provide and maintain alarms in such positions in any street or public place as they think proper;

(*d*) to employ the brigade or use the equipment outside their area;

(*e*) to employ the brigade or use the equipment for suitable

---

[11]It should be noticed also that except as regards factories, he can only demand entry if he has given the occupier twenty-four hours' notice of his intention to enter.

[12]The paragraph which is concerned with the securing of arrangements for the giving of advice.

[13]A lawyer would want to know more about this idea of efficiency. How efficient must efficient be?

purposes other than fire fighting purposes and, if it is thought fit, to charge for any service so rendered.

Again, this all seems quite clear and does not require further explanation, although a comment may be useful on the final para (*e*). The power given by para. (*e*) relates to what are known in the fire service as "special service calls" and would cover, for example, rescue work and the pumping of flooded premises. It is noteworthy, moreover, that there is included a power to charge for such services,[14] a point of interest inasmuch as one learns from s. 3(4) that basically a fire authority has no power to charge for the service which it provides.[15]

From the extensive scope of the fire authority's duties and powers it will be appreciated that its task is by no means a light one. Moreover, in order to ensure that the fire authority maintains a high standard, inspectors are appointed to keep a watch on the way in which it carries out its functions.

C. THE ESTABLISHMENT AND RUNNING OF FIRE BRIGADES

Looking back to s. 1(1) of the 1947 Act, one recalls that it places on every fire authority a duty to make provision for fire fighting purposes, and in particular, under s. 1(1)(*a*), to secure the services for their area of such a fire brigade and such equipment as may be necessary to meet efficiently all normal requirements.

The actual establishment of a fire brigade is determined in accordance with a scheme made by the fire authority, and the scheme is known quite simply, as an "establishment scheme". If the matters contained in an establishment scheme are investigated, it is found that they include fire stations, equipment, and personnel, (i.e., the number of members of a brigade, with reference to their descriptions and ranks). Obviously, such schemes must be fairly

---

[14]In practice, charges are confined to services of a non-humanitarian nature. To the question, "why should this be so?", one must answer that if the fire service were to engage in work which could otherwise be performed by a contractor, and not charge for it, the contractor could contend that the practice put in jeopardy his livelihood. Clearly, it is a different matter if a special service call is of an urgent nature where human or animal life is at risk: here the fire service will act immediately and without charge.

[15]This is a most important point, and emerges from the fact that the fire authority is under a duty to protect the public from danger.

flexible, but they must also be reasonably detailed, or there can be no certainty that the needs of the area are fulfilled.

Having dealt with the *establishment* of a fire brigade, we must pass next to the *running* of a fire brigade, and, in so doing, consider conditions of service, appointments, promotions, discipline and pensions. First, conditions of service:[16] these come within the purview of the National Joint Council for Local Authorities' Fire Brigades. From time to time this Council makes pronouncements upon various aspects of the matter, and it appears that they are accepted by most local authorities. Secondly, appointments and promotions: these, by contrast, fall within the province of the Secretary of State, who has power under s. 18 of the Act to make regulations concerning the same. Thirdly, the maintenance of discipline: this also is a matter for the Secretary of State, who is given a power of regulation by s. 17 of the Act. As the reader may be well aware, a code has been laid down for the express purpose of maintaining discipline. This code includes a list of disciplinary offences,[17] the procedure which must be followed both before a charge is heard and during its hearing, the punishments which can be meted out, and the rights of appeal which exist.[18] And finally, pensions: these too come within the control of the Secretary of State, who has power to make and vary what is known as a "firemen's pension scheme".

So much then, for the establishment and running of a fire brigade . . . In a little book of this nature there is not time to say more, but it is obvious from even this brief explanation that we have touched upon an activity of immense proportions and numerous facets. Now let us narrow the field somewhat, and consider:

D. THE SPECIAL POWERS GIVEN BY PARLIAMENT TO FIREMEN

Here attention must be paid to s. 30 of the 1947 Act, part of which is rather complicated and demands careful study.

Section 30(1) gives to any member of a fire brigade who is on duty, the right (in certain circumstances), to enter and if necessary

---

[16]Pay, leave, uniforms, etc.

[17]The "disciplinary offences" appear under headings, such as for example, disobedience to orders, neglect of duty, discreditable or disorderly conduct.

[18]Appeals are made to the fire authority or the Secretary of State.

to break into any premises or place,[19] and this he can do without the consent of the owner or occupier of those premises or place. What, then, are the circumstances in which he can exercise the right? We gather from the subsection that he can enter any premises or place in which either a fire has *actually* broken out, or is *reasonably believed* to have broken out. Again, he can enter any premises or place it is necessary to enter to put out a fire, or to protect the premises or place from acts done for fire fighting purposes. Moreover, proceeding still further through s. 30(1) we find that not only may the fireman enter the premises or place, but after having so entered, is entitled to do certain acts. Thus, he can do all he thinks necessary to put out a fire, to rescue any person or property, to protect the premises or place from fire, or to protect the premises or place from acts done for fire fighting purposes.[20]

These are, it is clear, extensive rights of entry, but no-one would question the need for them in the circumstances in question.

Passing from s. 30(1) to s. 30(5) we find rights given to certain fire officers; rights which have to be given if they are to cope efficiently with the emergency of fire. Thus, sub-s. (5) explains that if there is no police officer present at a fire, the senior officer of the fire brigade who is present can close to traffic any street, or stop or regulate traffic in any street, if it is necessary or desirable so to do for fire fighting purposes. (One sees that it is the senior officer present who is given these rights; he it is one learns from s. 30(3) of the Act who has at any fire the sole charge and control of all operations for the extinction of the fire.) Finally, it should be kept in mind that not only is the chief officer present at a fire given the right to interfere with the flow of traffic, but also the right to interfere with the supply of water to the public. In this respect it is from s. 30(4) one gathers that if a senior fire brigade officer present at a fire asks those who control the supply of water for a greater supply and pressure of water, the latter must take all

---

[19]Note that the right is given to any member of a fire brigade who is *on duty*. The section also enables a constable to break and enter, but makes no mention at all of whether or not the constable is on duty.

[20]It is interesting (at least to a lawyer), to notice that s. 30(1) gives the fireman on duty the right, having entered any premises or place, to do all he thinks necessary to protect the premises or place from fire, or to rescue any person or property, but it does not give him, *in the first place*, an express right to enter for either of those purposes.

the necessary steps to comply with the requirements, and in an effort to comply, may shut off water from the mains and pipes in any area.

(Finally, while dealing with the powers given by Parliament to firemen, one should consider also the way in which special privileges are afforded to fire appliances. Thus, under s. 18 of the Road Traffic Act 1960, a vehicle may be driven elsewhere than on a road if it is so driven for the purpose of saving life or extinguishing fire, and, under s. 25 of the same Act, any vehicle which is being used for fire brigade purposes is exempt from any speed limit imposed, if the observance of the limit would hinder the use of the vehicle. Again, under reg. 89 of the Motor Vehicles (Construction and Use) Regulations 1966, vehicles used for fire brigade purposes are exempt from restrictions on the use of audible warning instruments, and, under reg. 94, from restrictions on the standing of vehicles on the road during the hours of darkness. And last of all, the Road Vehicles Lighting Regulations 1959 (as amended in 1961), vary a provision of the Road Transport Lighting Act 1957, so that vehicles used for fire fighting purposes can carry a flashing blue light or lights).

So much then for the granting by Parliament of special rights, all of which are designed to protect people and property at times of urgent need. Now let us turn to what may well be thought the most pressing of all matters connected with "fire fighting purposes", namely,

E. THE SUPPLY OF WATER

As regards the supply of water, the story begins with s. 13 of the 1947 Act. This section says a fire authority shall take all reasonable measures for ensuring the provision of an adequate supply of water, and for securing its availability for use in case of fire. Again, therefore we meet a section which imposes a *duty*. How, though, is the fire authority to fulfil this duty? To find the answer one turns to ss. 14 and 15 of the Act.

Section 14 says that a fire authority may enter into an agreement with statutory water undertakers[1] for the latter to take measures

---

[1]Who or what are *statutory water undertakers*? In general terms, a statutory water undertaker is any company, local authority, board, committee or other person *authorised* to supply water.

to secure the availability of an adequate water supply in the event of fire. So far as the *adequacy of the supply* is concerned, one gathers that fire authorities tend to take the view that in "high risk" areas of factories or large shops they can only meet their responsibility to ensure an adequate supply if the water undertaking have adequate mains and supplies to those mains. It is not considered that the fire authority should go to the huge expense of causing a special main to be laid.

Looking further ahead one should note that the section expressly mentions the inclusion in the agreement of terms as to payment or otherwise, and further provides that no water undertaker can reasonably refuse to enter into such an agreement.

Section 15(1) adds to all this by giving the fire authority power to secure by agreement, the use, in the event of fire, of water which is under the control of somebody other than statutory water undertakers; while, finally, apart from the power given by s. 15(1), s. 15(2) gives the authority power to use for fire fighting purposes any convenient and suitable supply of water.[2]

All in all, therefore, provision is made for the availability of an adequate water supply in every possible way; no source is left untapped.

To conclude this note on the supply of water mention must be made of *fire hydrants*:[3]

At the request of the fire authority, statutory water undertakers must provide and fix fire hydrants on their mains. Further, they must fix them at places which are most convenient to afford a supply to extinguish any fire which breaks out within the limits of the undertakers' supply. So to do, though, is not the end of the matter: the undertakers must also keep them in good order and clearly indicate their situation by a notice or distinguishing mark. Moreover, as soon as a hydrant is completed, the undertakers must, at the fire authority's request, deposit a key to it at each place (within the limits of the supply) where a public fire appliance is kept.

To provide, fix, maintain and indicate the site of hydrants, and

---

[2] There is the point though, that reasonable compensation must be paid.
[3] Here we stray from the 1947 Act to the Water Act 1945. See the Third Schedule, Part VIII, beginning with s. 32.

to deposit keys to the same, is, of course, an expensive business. The expense in each instance is borne, however, by the fire authority.

CONCLUSION

In just a few pages we have touched upon the principal features of the organisation of a fire fighting service. There have been considered in turn the way in which the service is set up, the duties and powers of fire authorities, the establishment and running of fire brigades, the special rights given to firemen, and the supply of water. In so doing, we have had cause to deal with many and varied matters, but there is nevertheless a strong link which forges them together and gives them coherence. Very simply it is: the need to provide an efficient service, ready to cope at any time with the sudden emergency of fire.

Chapter 3

FIRE PRECAUTIONS

INTRODUCTION

In this chapter we shall be concerned exclusively with the law relating to fire precautions. It is an area of law composed entirely of legislation and delegated legislation, and, for historical reasons it is one which is far from easy to study.

The fundamental difficulty lies in the fact that it is a branch of law which has grown up over a long period of time in a piecemeal fashion. As the need for legislative control has arisen in any particular context, so it has been met, with the consequence that the overall picture is one of innumerable, scattered enactments which impinge upon the most diverse topics, the only link being that each is concerned, amongst other things, with the risk of fire. Such indeed is the diversity of the topics involved, that one can find sections on fire precautions in legislation dealing for instance with factories, education, consumer protection, explosives, pet animals, housing, betting and gaming, petroleum and nursing homes, and this is to take but a random selection!

During the past few years this state of affairs has given rise to considerable criticism, and not least for the point that the piece-meal development resulted in the lack of a uniform system of responsibility for enforcement. Increasingly, there has been a demand for all the law on fire precautions to be consolidated into a single, comprehensive piece of legislation, and while its very diversity would have rendered impracticable such a venture, there has recently appeared a new Act, the Fire Precautions Act

1971, which should eventually do much to rationalise and strengthen the existing law, and to bring under proper control premises which have hitherto escaped. It must not be thought, however (and the point is emphasised at this early stage), that the Fire Precautions Act will one day render obsolete all the other legislation relating to fire precautions: far from it. Some of it will be rendered obsolete, but a great portion will remain; for example, it will not affect the legislation which relates to fire precautions in factories, offices, shops and railway premises.

In view of these circumstances, it is proposed to study this sphere of law by dealing in turn with the more important of the many and varied enactments which deal, amongst other matters, with fire precautions, and to postpone to the end of the chapter a treatment of the Fire Precautions Act.

(i) *The Factories Act* 1961

This Act, which impinges upon the daily lives of millions, is designed to promote the safety, health and welfare of those who work in factories. It is a huge and intricate piece of legislation, and made effective by the elaborate organisation of a factory inspectorate. Obviously, fire precautions are amongst its chief objectives. . .

Whenever one is dealing with the Factories Act, however, the first thing to do is to make sure one understands what is meant by a "factory". In s. 175(1) there is a long definition of a factory, but it comes, briefly, to this: A factory is a place in which persons are employed for the purpose of making, treating or altering articles, or of slaughtering animals. In any event, the work must be manual, and carried on for the purpose of gain.

Bearing in mind then what is meant by a "factory", what does the Act have to say regarding fire therein? Its fundamental concern is with means of escape. Thus, we learn from s. 40 that certain premises may not be used as a factory unless there is in force a fire certificate from the fire authority that the premises are provided with such means of escape in case of fire as may reasonably be required.[1] (Although it should be noticed that there

---

[1]Notice that it is the *fire authority* who gives the certificate. While it is the factory inspectorate which carries the main burden of rendering the Act effective, there are, in this respect, other persons who also have duties cast upon them. Here we find a duty cast upon fire authorities.

is no prohibition on use between the time when an application for a certificate is made and the time the certificate is granted or refused.) To the question, "what type of premises require such a certificate?" we find an answer in s.45. In general terms we can gather from that section that they are premises in which either more than twenty persons are employed, or in which more than ten persons are employed at certain levels above ground level,[2] or in which there are kept explosive or highly inflammable materials.

Before a fire authority will grant a certificate, it carries out an examination of the premises involved, and has to be satisfied that there are reasonable means of escape. Moreover, the authority is empowered to require that alterations to premises shall be made as a condition of granting a certificate.[3] So far as the certificate itself is concerned, s. 40(6) provides that it must contain certain precise information. This is information as to the means of escape provided, the maximum number of persons employed in the factory, the existence in the factory of explosive or highly inflammable material, and any other matters taken into account on the granting of a certificate.

So much then for certification by the fire authority; but that is by no means the end of the matter. Turning next to s. 48 we find further provisions expressly designed to safeguard employees from fire. They are provisions, moreover, of diverse kinds, and space forbids more than a brief summary survey. Thus, amongst other things, s. 48 provides that doors shall not be locked or fastened in such a way that they cannot be easily and immediately opened from the inside; that doors (other than sliding doors) providing an exit from the building shall be made to open outwards; that windows, doors or other exits affording means of escape in case of fire other than exits which are not in ordinary use must be conspicuously marked; that hoistways or liftways

[2]It is worth noting at this point that when we come to deal with the Offices, Shops and Railway Premises Act 1963 (a later Act than the Factories Act) we shall find reference, in s. 29, to "more than ten persons being employed elsewhere than on the ground floor". The impact of this is to bring basements into control which are not controllable under the parallel provision in the Factories Act.

[3]Section 43 gives any occupier of a factory a right to appeal to a magistrates' court if he is aggrieved by the refusal of a fire authority to grant a certificate, or by a requirement to carry out alterations.

31

must be enclosed with fire-resisting materials; that the contents of rooms must be so arranged as to provide free passage-way for persons employed in the room to a means of escape in case of fire; and that effective means must be provided and maintained for giving audible warning in case of fire.[4]

Even then we must continue still further: s. 49 provides that in factories where either more than twenty persons are employed at certain levels above ground level, or there are kept explosive or highly inflammable materials, effective steps must be taken to make sure employees are familiar with the means of escape in case of fire. And yet again, s. 51 tells us that in every factory there must be provided and maintained appropriate means for fighting fire, which shall be so placed as to be readily available for use.

These, then, are amongst the most important provisions on fire prevention in factories; space does not permit of further details, but from the points made, the policy of the Act as regards fire emerges clearly.

(ii) *The Offices, Shops and Railway Premises Act* 1963

The concern of the Offices, Shops and Railway Premises Act, like that of the Factories Act, is with the safety, health and welfare of people at work. Moreover, it is not only identity of object which links the two Acts, but also similarity of approach. Thus, for instance, the fire precaution provisions of the 1963 Act are presented in a pattern which follows fairly closely that of the 1961 Act...

Once again, attention is focused primarily upon means of escape. Section 29 makes it unlawful to employ (*a*) more than twenty persons in premises to which the Act applies, or (*b*) more than ten persons elsewhere than on the ground floor of any such premises, or (*c*) any persons in any such premises if explosive or highly inflammable materials are kept, *unless*, with respect to those premises, there is in force a "fire certificate", issued by the

---

[4]Section 52 provides for periodical testing or examination of every means for giving warning in case of fire.

appropriate authority,[5] that the premises are provided with such means of escape as may reasonably be required. (Notice once more, though, that there is no prohibition between the time of applying for such a certificate and the time of its being granted or refused.) As in the case of factories, the fire certificate contains a number of specific matters, viz: the greatest number of people who can safely be employed in the premises, the means of escape provided, and any special fire risks which are inherent in the premises.[6] Section 30 then takes up the tale by requiring that all means of escape specified in a fire certificate be properly maintained and kept free from obstruction, and s. 36 continues it still further by requiring that effective steps be taken to ensure employees are familiar with the means of escape provided.

Turning next to ss. 33 and 34 we find still more provisions which echo those of the Factories Act. Thus, s. 33(1) provides that doors through which an employee might have to pass to get out of the premises shall not be so locked or fastened, that they cannot be immediately opened by him; s. 33(2) provides that the contents of rooms shall be so arranged as to afford persons working in the room free passage-way to a means of escape; and s. 33(3) requires that exits other than those in ordinary use be distinctively and conspicuously marked. Section 34, though, confines itself to fire alarms. Section 34(1) requires that all the premises involved shall be provided with effective means of giving warning in case of fire, while s. 34(2) requires that the means of giving warning shall be tested or examined at least once every three months.

Last but not least there remains for consideration s. 38 of the Act. This section, like s. 51 of the Factories Act requires the provision and maintenance of appropriate means for fighting fire, these means to be so placed as to be readily available for use.

So, let us sum up on the 1963 Act. If the reader looks at the Act, he will see that from amongst the most important sections on fire precautions there have been selected those which give a

---

[5]The appropriate authority is generally the fire authority, but in certain circumstances may be the factory inspectorate. The latter is the case, for example, in respect of premises owned or occupied by the Crown, premises occupied by fire and police authorities and premises in a school maintained by a local education authority.
[6]Again, as in the case of factories, premises have to be investigated and, where necessary, alterations effected, before a certificate is granted.

general picture of the approach adopted by Parliament to the problems presented by the threat of fire. Necessarily, the picture which emerges bears strong resemblance to that which emerges from the Factories Act 1961.

Many of the problems which arise in connection with factories, offices and shops, etc., stem from the fact that they are premises in which people assemble; and it is with the dangers inherent in such assembly that we are concerned in the next Act:

(iii) *The Public Health Act* 1936[7]

This Act, like the two preceding Acts, is a lengthy and complex affair, and only certain of its sections are devoted to fire precautions. Section 59 of the Act is directed to the need for satisfactory exits and entrances in places where members of the public assemble. Its provisions apply to a wide range of such places, including theatres, halls, stores, restaurants, clubs, schools and places of public worship; and it deals with the problem by treating separately buildings which *it is proposed to build*, and buildings which are *already in existence*. With regard to the former, a duty is placed on local authorities to reject plans of buildings within the section, unless it is shown that they are to be provided with satisfactory means of ingress and egress, passages or gangways.[8] Again, with regard to the latter, if it is found that any such building is not provided with satisfactory[9] means of ingress and egress, passages or gangways, the local authority must require the owner of the building to remedy the defect by carrying out the necessary work. Having dealt with the matter of satisfactory provision, the section then deals with the matter of freedom from obstruction. Thus, sub-s. (4) requires the person who has control of the building to take steps to secure that the means of ingress and egress and the passages or gangways are kept free and unobstructed while people are assembled in the building. Attention must be drawn, furthermore, to the final few words of this requirement, namely, *"while people are assembled in the building"*; clearly, this is an important aspect of the matter.

---

[7]Attention may be drawn to the point that eventually the Fire Precautions Act 1971 will have enormous impact upon this portion of fire precautions legislation.

[8]Whether or not they are "satisfactory" relates to the purpose for which the building is to be used, and the number of persons likely to resort to it at any one time.

[9]See footnote 8 above.

Turning next to s. 60, we find that it is directed to means of escape from fire in certain high buildings. Subsection (1) of s. 60 provides that where it appears to a local authority that an existing or proposed building within the section is not, or will not be, provided with such means of escape from floors more than twenty feet above the ground as the authority thinks necessary, the authority shall require either the owner of the building, or the persons who propose to erect the building, to carry out the necessary work. So the question now arises, what are the high buildings which fall within the section? The answer to this question appears in sub-s. (4) of s. 60. In general terms, sub-s. (4) says that s. 60 applies to any building of more than two storeys, in which the floor of any upper storey is more than twenty feet from the ground on any side of the building, and which is either (a) let out in flats, or (b) used as an inn, hotel, boarding house, nursing home, boarding school, or similar institution, or (c) used as a restaurant, shop or store, and has on any upper floor sleeping accommodation for employees.

Our final concern with the fire precautions aspect of the Public Health Act lies with ss. 61 and 62; but here we must proceed on a cautious note, because changes have been made with regard to these sections by the *Public Health Act* 1961.

Section 61 of the 1936 Act has been a section of great importance and wide impact, not only from the fire prevention point of view, but from every aspect of public health and safety. It enabled local authorities to make what were known as "building bye-laws", so giving them power to regulate the construction of buildings in their respective areas. Moreover, by regulation is meant *detailed* regulation, encompassing not only fire measures, but also such matters as requirements relating to space, light, ventilation, height and sanitation facilities. Section 62 then carried the business a stage further by empowering local authorities to make bye-laws governing alterations to and the change of use of buildings.

Over a number of years, however, these sections proved cumbersome, and a trouble to local authorities and builders alike. Accordingly, in 1961 a fundamental change was effected. Section 4 of the Public Health Act of that year removed from local authorities the power to make building bye-laws. Henceforth, the building bye-laws were to be replaced by centrally made "building regulations". It is important to notice, though, that while the power to make building bye-laws has been removed from the local authorities, they remain, nevertheless, the authorities responsible for the administration and enforcement of the centrally made building regulations.[10]

So much then for the Public Health Acts of 1936 and 1961 . . . Next we must turn our attention to legislation which is concerned exclusively with dangerous residences, dealing first with the Caravan Sites and Control of Development Act 1960.

(iv) *The Caravan Sites and Control of Development Act* 1960

The safety, health and welfare of the inhabitants of caravan sites naturally give rise to special problems, not least amongst which is the problem of fire. Obviously, caravan sites must be subjected to some measure of control, and if one takes a look at the 1960 Act one finds that control is achieved by means of a licensing system which is administered by local authorities and supervised by a central authority.[11] In this context, s. 5 of the Act demands one's attention, for it provides, *inter alia*, that when a local authority issues a site licence it may impose such conditions as it thinks necessary or desirable in the interests of the persons dwelling on the site. Moreover, so far as fire is concerned, the local authority may in particular impose conditions for securing that "proper measures are taken for preventing and detecting the outbreak of fire and adequate means of fighting fire are provided and maintained".

Again, if one delves more deeply into s. 5, one sees that provision is made for the central authority to specify "model standards" with respect to the layout of sites, and the provision of facilities, services and equipment, and that local authorities, when deciding what conditions to attach to a site licence, shall have regard to such standards. In 1960, model standards were issued for residential caravan sites, and contained express provision for fire fighting appliances. Thus, the relevant paragraph reads as follows:

---

[10]It is noteworthy that in England (unlike in Scotland), the fire precautions measures contained in the regulations do not include provision for means of escape.

[11]Mention should be made of the fact that fairground caravans are exempt from control by licensing.

"Where there is a water supply of sufficient pressure and flow, there should be a fire hydrant to conform with B.S.S. 750 within 300 feet of every caravan standing. Fire points, each equipped with a water tank provided with a hinged cover, two buckets and one hand pump or bucket pump, should be provided on the scale of one point for every two acres or part of two acres. On sites with no hydrants, each water tank should contain at least 100 gallons of water. The fire points should be clearly marked and easily accessible in case of fire."

Secondly, one must look at the Housing Act 1961, and certain Housing Regulations made in 1962, for one is concerned also with residences which, from the point of view of fire, are equally as dangerous as caravans, viz., houses in multiple occupation:

(v) *The Housing Act* 1961

In this Act one finds a number of sections relating to houses which are in multiple occupation, i.e., houses which are let in lodgings, or are occupied by the members of more than one family. After making provision for ensuring that such houses are kept in a satisfactory state by the persons who manage them, the Act then passes from the general matter of proper management to the more particular matter of means of escape from fire. In s. 16 it is provided that if a local authority finds such a house lacks the means of escape which the authority thinks necessary, the authority may serve a notice on the person who manages the house. The notice specifies the work which is necessary to provide a proper means of escape, and requires him to execute it. Furthermore, s. 18 provides that if the person should fail to comply with the notice, the local authority can undertake the work and recover reasonable expenses. The story is not complete, however, without a reference to the Housing Regulations 1961 which apply to houses in multiple occupation.[12] Regulation 10 provides that a person who manages such a house shall make sure that all means of escape from fire in the house are kept in proper repair and free from obstruction.

So much, then, for the fire risks inherent in dangerous resi-

---

[12]S.I. 1962 No. 668.

dences. . . . Next, we must concern ourselves with the fire risks present in places of entertainment and social resort, i.e., in cinemas, theatres, clubs, and so on. First on the list come cinemas:

(vi) *The Cinematograph Acts* 1909 *and* 1952 *and the Cinematograph (Safety) Regulations* 1955[13]

The main concern here is with the Regulations, but a preliminary word is necessary about the two Acts: The Cinematograph Act 1909 requires cinemas to be licensed, and enables the Secretary of State to make regulations in respect of them. For some years, this Act applied only where inflammable film was used, but the Cinematograph Act 1952 extended it so as to make it apply to most of the cinematograph exhibitions given in England and Wales, *regardless of the type of film used*. With this in mind then, let us consider the Regulations which have been made, their object being to provide a detailed safety code for cinemas.

If one glances at the Regulations, one notices that they are arranged in a number of separate parts, and for present purposes our interest lies in Parts 1, 2 and 3: The provisions of Part 1 apply to all cinematograph exhibitions (with the exception of certain noncommercial exhibitions), unless they fall within the scope of Part 3. Part 3, which contains less rigid rules than Part 1, applies to cinematograph exhibitions (again excluding certain noncommercial exhibitions), which are given in places like village halls, i.e., in small premises which are only used occasionally for such a purpose. It should be noticed, though, that the less stringent provisions of Part 3 *do not apply* if there is any inflammable film on the premises. Finally, Part 2 contains provisions which apply *in addition to those contained in Part* 1, whenever the giving of the exhibition *involves the use of inflammable film*.[14] Keeping in mind, then, the arrangement of the Regulations, let us consider the portions which are directly concerned with fire precautions. . .

Beginning with Part 1 of the Regulations, we must first deal with reg. 2. This requires that premises be provided with an

---

[13]These regulations appear as S.I. 1955 No. 1129.
[14]There is no need to concern oneself with these provisions, though, if the exhibition is given in a private dwelling-house and the public is not admitted.

adequate number of clearly indicated exits so placed and maintained as to afford the public safe egress. Further, it requires that
all doors open easily (and generally, *outwards*), and that all
passages and stairways be kept free from obstruction. Thus,
once again, we find that the principal interest, logically enough,
is in *escape*. Regulation 5 then continues the tale with a number
of varied requirements, all of which involve precautions against
fire. Thus, in general terms, it requires (1) that the premises be
provided with fire appliances suitable to the fire risks in the
premises; (2) that those appliances be properly maintained and
available for immediate use; (3) that the licensee[15] and certain
members of his staff be properly instructed with regard to protecting the premises from fire; (4) that curtains be so treated as not
readily to catch fire; and (5) that no inflammable substance be
used to clean film or projectors. Again, reg. 6 takes matters
further by forbidding smoking in certain parts of the cinema,[16]
and by requiring the posting of notices to that effect. Turning
then to reg. 12, we find a less obvious but equally vital requirement,
viz., that holes by which pipes, ducts or conductors pass through
a fire-resisting wall, floor or ceiling must be so sealed as to
prevent the passage of fire and smoke.

And finally, to conclude Part 1, we pass to reg. 24. Amongst
other things, this regulation requires that heating appliances
situated within reach of the public be fixed in position and fitted
with a guard; that such appliances be situated sufficiently far from
materials or substances liable to catch fire for there to be no
likelihood of fire; and that such appliances situated in a projection
or rewinding room be so constructed as there to be no likelihood
of film igniting.

Part 3, it will be recalled, contains the less stringent provisions
designed to apply to small premises used only occasionally for
cinematograph exhibitions, so long as no inflammable film is
present; and in this regard our concern is with regs. 36 and 39.
First, regulation 36: This regulation, like reg. 2 in Part 1, is involved with the provision of exits. Like reg. 2, it requires (i) that
the premises be provided with adequate and clearly indicated

---

[15]I.e., the recipient of the licence for the cinema.
[16]Such as, for instance, the projection room, or rooms where film is stored.

39

exits, so placed as to afford the public safe egress, and (ii) that the passages and stairways be kept clear from obstruction. Unlike reg. 2, though, it does not impose requirements as to the construction of doors. *Secondly, regulation* 39: This regulation, like regs. 5 and 6 of Part 1, is concerned with fire precautions, but again its requirements are not so harsh. Thus it requires (1) that fire appliances suitable to the fire risks in the premises be provided; (2) that those appliances be properly maintained and available for immediate use; (3) that no inflammable substance be used for cleaning films or projectors; and (4) that any metal work of a projector liable to become charged with electricity if a defect should occur, be effectively earthed.

Part 2, it has been mentioned, contains provisions which are to apply in addition to those of Part 1, whenever the giving of the exhibition involves the use of inflammable film. The regulations of this Part are all extremely detailed, and reflect naturally the special dangers of their subject-matter. Thus, reg. 30 sets the tenor of the whole of Part 2. It reads: "All persons employed in connection with cinematograph exhibitions who may be called upon to handle or use inflammable film shall be warned of the special dangers attaching to inflammable film and shall be instructed in the special precautions . . . which should be taken in . . . its handling and use." Regulation 31 then takes up the theme by requiring, amongst other things, that the walls, floors, ceilings and doors of the projection and rewinding rooms be so constructed or lined as to be fire-resisting, and, moreover, that in these rooms all the fittings, fixtures, furniture and furnishings be of such material or so treated as not readily to catch fire. And yet again, regs. 32, 33 and 34 continue in the same vein. Relating respectively to the construction of spools and spool-boxes, the keeping and use of inflammable film, and the equipping of projection and rewinding rooms, each regulation imposes strict requirements for the prevention of fire.

From all these many provisions it will be apparent that the danger of fire at cinematograph exhibitions has been afforded considerable attention, due, of course, to the high degree of risk which is involved. So much then, for the risk of fire in cinemas; our next concern is with the risk of fire in theatres, and here we must begin with:

(vii) *The Theatres Act* 1968

The object of this Act is to bring theatres under a strict measure of control, and this object is achieved in a number of lengthy and detailed provisions. Our interest lies, however, in just one of these provisions, namely s. 12. One of the most significant sections of the Act, it provides that no premises are to be used for the public performance of any play except in accordance with the terms of a licence granted by the licensing authority.

The "licensing authority" from which the licensee obtains his licence is the local authority, and the licensee has to comply with the terms which the local authority inserts. Again, "regulations" are made by local authorities for the management of theatres, and the observance of these regulations is made a term of the licence. From the fire point of view the regulations are vital, for much of them are directed to fire precautions; but inasmuch as they are made locally, they vary to some extent, from area to area. Even so, it is important that we should pay brief attention to one such set of regulations, in order to appreciate the sort of points of which are taken. By way of illustration, therefore, there has been chosen a set which apply in a certain large, provincial city:

(viii) *Locally made regulations for theatre management*

As regards fire prevention, the chief features of these particular regulations are their wide scope and minute detail. They require so many precautions to be taken, and define them with such precision, that in a short space one can only list the more important amongst them:

The primary concern is, as ever, with escape:[17] thus, the regulations require amongst other things the seats to be fixed, the external doors to be constructed so that they open outwards, the exits and gangways to be kept free from obstruction, and the size of audience to be so restricted as to avoid danger from overcrowding. Passing from problems of escape to those of fire itself, the regulations list amongst their requirements the possession by the theatre of direct telephonic communication with

---

[17]It should be kept in mind also that s. 59 of the Public Health Act 1936 requires the provision of satisfactory exits and entrances in theatres.

the fire brigade, and, during any stage performance, the constant presence of a trained fireman. Moreover, if there should be any outbreak of fire, the regulations require information of it to be communicated immediately to the fire brigade. Further, there must be provided and maintained throughout the premises appropriate means and equipment for fighting fire, and all scenery, draperies, properties and the like must be non-inflammable, and the safety curtain must be maintained in good working order.

These then, are amongst the more important requirements relating to fire prevention in the theatre. All in all, the regulations, place a heavy burden on the licensee, who is given the full re sponsibility for carrying them out. . .

In dealing with fire in places of entertainment there have so far been considered the cinema and the large, commercial theatre. It must not be forgotten, however, that music and dancing promoted for gain often take place in smaller, private premises, and that in these circumstances also a fire risk emerges due to the assembly of numbers of persons. The need to control such gatherings is met by:

(ix) *The Private Places of Entertainment (Licensing) Act* 1967

Under this Act premises used for public music or dancing are licensed. Again, the licensing is a local matter, licences being issued by local "licensing" authorities, and held on their terms. Further, the fire prevention aspect is taken care of by means of inspection of any premises for which a licence is sought.

Our next concern, in the sphere of places of entertainment and social resort, is with clubs, restaurants, and guest houses, and particularly with regard to the sale in such places of intoxicating liquor. Control over them is exercised by the now familiar process of licensing, and the law on the matter is contained in:

(x) *The Licensing Act* 1964

Putting aside for a moment the sale of intoxicating liquor in restaurants and guest houses, let us first consider its sale in clubs. From s. 39 of the Act one learns that any club wishing to sell intoxicating liquor to its members must either hold a justices' licence, or have a registration certificate issued by the justices for the area. When a club makes an application to the justices for permission to sell intoxicating liquor, a copy of the application is sent to the fire authority, and s. 46 gives that authority the right to enter and inspect the premises involved, *with regard to any matter affecting fire risk*. Moreover, the fire authority may object to the granting of permission on the ground that the premises are not suitable and convenient for the purpose, in view of their character and condition, and of the size and nature of the club.[18] Similarly, it is necessary for those who run restaurants and guest houses to acquire a licence if they wish to sell intoxicating liquor to their customers, and if the justices consider the premises are not suitable and convenient having regard to their character and condition, and to the extent of the proposed use, they may refuse the application.[19] Thus, for instance, no licence may be granted, if from an inspection of the premises undertaken by the fire authority, it appears that the premises are unsuitable from the point of view of fire.

So much, then, for the Licensing Act 1964, from which we must turn to the Gaming Act 1968, the last Act for consideration in this particular sphere.

(xi) *The Gaming Act* 1968

Here our interest centres on the control (from the fire prevention aspect) exerted over commercial gaming establishments, and, once again, we find that resort is had to the process of licensing.

Applications are made for licences to the justices, and copies of such applications are sent to the fire authorities, If, then, from the aspect of fire prevention, the premises in any particular instance are unsuitable in their layout, character, condition or location, a licence may be refused. And equally, a licence may be refused if the fire authority has not been given reasonable facilities to inspect the premises. Again, if application is made for the *renewal* of a licence it may fail if appropriate precautions against the danger of fire have not been observed, or have been insufficiently observed.

---

[18]See s. 44 of the Act.
[19]See s. 98 of the Act.

Of course, if fire authorities are to protect the public in this field, they must have express power under the Act to enter and inspect any premises involved. Such power is afforded by s. 43(*a*) of the Act, which provides that any person authorised by the fire authority in whose area the premises are situated, may, at any reasonable time enter the premises for the purpose of ascertaining whether appropriate precautions against the danger of fire are being sufficiently observed.

Next we must look at a brief provision, which rather stands apart from the material we have so far considered:

(xii) *Section 11, Children and Young Persons Act 1933 (as amended by s. 8, Children and Young Persons Amendment Act 1952)*

This section makes criminally liable a person of sixteen or over who has the care of a child under twelve, and causes that child's death or serious injury by allowing him in a room which contains an open fire grate, or a heating appliance liable to injure, and by taking no reasonable precautions to prevent burning or scalding.

Immediately obvious are the limitations of this legislation inasmuch as it contemplates the child's "death or serious injury".

Turning then from dangerous premises, circumstances and conditions, to dangerous *substances*, we come to the legislation and delegated legislation which governs the handling and use of petroleum spirit and other inflammable liquids. Unfortunately, it is a complicated area of the law, but this is understandable inasmuch as the high degree of risk involved calls for the most detailed control.

(xiii) *The Petroleum (Consolidation) Act 1928*

Section 1(1) of the Petroleum (Consolidation) Act 1928, brings under control the *keeping* of petroleum spirit. It says that petrol shall not be kept unless there is in force a "petroleum spirit licence" authorising its keeping. Straightaway, however, there appears an exception. Section 1(1) goes on to say that petrol may be kept without a licence so long as, (*a*) it is kept in separate glass, earthenware or metal vessels, securely stopped and containing not more than one pint each, *and* (*b*) the whole amount kept, in bulk, would not be more than three gallons. Obviously, the danger

44

is minimised if only a small quantity is kept, and it is kept in suitable containers.

From s. 1 one proceeds to s. 10 of the Act, which enables the Secretary of State to make regulations as to the keeping and use of petrol by people *intending to use it for motor vehicles*. Under this section there have been made regulations which are known as the *Petroleum-Spirit (Motor Vehicles, etc.) Regulations* 1929,[20] and these we must now consider:

(xiv) *The Petroleum-Spirit (Motor Vehicles, etc.) Regulations* 1929

Regulation 1 provides that where people keep and use petrol for such purposes as motor vehicles, motor boats, aircraft, lawnmowers, stationary generators and the like[1] (and do not keep it for sale), it must be kept and used in accordance with the regulations. In this regard it is important to notice that s. 1 of the 1928 Act has nothing to do with the matter, for, in technical language, the keeping and use of petrol for these purposes is "exempt" from the requirements of that section. While therefore a licence is not necessary where petrol is kept and used for these purposes, the measure of control is nevertheless strict:

Beginning with regs. 2, 3 and 4, we find that the petrol must be kept in secure metal vessels, and conspicuously marked "petroleum spirit, highly inflammable". Moreover, no person may repair those vessels unless he has first taken care to see that they are free from spirit and vapour.

Regulation 5 then picks up the theme by imposing requirements as to the construction of storage places. In general terms, a storage place must be effectively ventilated, it must possess an entrance direct from the open air, and it must contain fire extinguishing apparatus. Again, it must not form part of a building which is used as a dwelling house or place of public resort, unless it is separated by a substantial floor or partition. And yet again, if it is in a building, unless it is separated in the ways just mentioned, it must not be situated under any means of escape.

---

[20]These regulations appear as S.R. & O.1929 No. 952. (Instruments made under statutory authority from 1894 to 1947 were generally registered as Statutory Rules and Orders—hence S.R. & O. After 1947, though, they appear as Statutory Instruments).

[1]For the complete list see reg. 1 and the Schedule.

45

Having dealt with containers and storage places, the regulations then move on to the matter of the *quantity kept*. From reg. 6 it appears that not more than sixty gallons of petrol may be kept at the same time in any one storage place. Here, though, there are two odd small points to notice. First, in adding up the sixty gallons which can be kept, one is obliged to take into account any petrol which is carried by any motor vehicle, motor boat or aircraft in the storage place. And secondly, if a person has two storage places which are less than twenty feet apart they count as one storage place only. Still on the matter of quantities, reg. 7 goes on to say that petrol may not be kept in any vessel *which holds more than two gallons*, unless (*a*) it is kept in a storage place more than twenty feet from buildings, highways or footpaths, and (*b*) provision has been made to prevent it escaping in the event of fire, and (*c*) the local authority has been advised of the intention so to keep it. Again, though, there is still a further small point to notice: When reg. 7 says that petrol may not be kept in vessels holding more than two gallons unless certain conditions are complied with, it expressly excludes the fuel tanks of motor vehicles, motor boats and aircraft. Lastly, in regard to quantities kept, we have to turn to reg. 8. This regulation tells us that petrol in a storage place which is situated within twenty feet of a building or inflammable substance, cannot generally be kept otherwise than (*a*) in the fuel tank of any motor vehicle, motor boat or aircraft, and (*b*) in not more than two other vessels each of two gallon capacity which are carried by such vehicle or craft.[2]

Our final concern with these regulations is with regs. 9, 10, 11 and 12, each of which involves precautions. Thus, regs. 9 and 10 require precautions to be taken in storage places to prevent the ignition of inflammable vapour. Again, reg. 11 provides that other than fuel used for lighting, heating, and (in very small quantities), cleaning purposes, petrol in any storage place shall only be used as fuel for a motor vehicle, motor boat or aircraft. And yet again, reg. 12 prohibits the emptying of petrol into sewers or drains.

So much, then, for the Petroleum-Spirit (Motor Vehicles, etc.)

---

[2] I say "generally" for the reason that if it is desired in such conditions to keep petrol in any other way, reg. 8 requires notice to be given to the local authority.

Regulations 1929; the power to make which, it will be recalled is found in s. 10 of the Petroleum (Consolidation) Act 1928. Turning next to s. 6 of the same Act, we find it gives power to the Secretary of State to make regulations regarding the conveyance of petrol by road. Regulations have been made under s. 6 which are known as the Petroleum-Spirit (Conveyance by Road) Regulations 1957;[3] and these must now be considered:

(xv) *The Petroleum-Spirit (Conveyance by Road) Regulations 1957 (as slightly amended by the Petroleum-Spirit (Conveyance by Road) Regulations 1958)*

These regulations are divided into a number of Parts; our concern being with certain aspects of Part 1 (which deals with general matters), Part 11 (which covers the conveyance of petrol in tank wagons or tank trailers;, and Part 111 (which covers conveyance of petrol in vehicles other than of those varieties).

So first let us consider the relevant portions of Part 1. From reg. 1 we learn that the regulations do not apply if not more than thirty two gallons of petrol are being conveyed in securely closed containers of fairly small capacity,[4] or if not more than fifty gallons are conveyed in a single, securely closed steel barrel. (As it has been seen, the crucial matters are the *quantity* of petrol involved and the type of container used.) Subject to these exceptions, then, the regulations apply.

As mentioned above, Part 1 is concerned with matters of a general kind, and regulations two to six list a number of fundamental requirements. Thus, regulations two and three require that people engaged in conveying, loading, and unloading petrol shall observe all the necessary precautions to prevent fire and to ensure that petrol does not enter any sewer or drain. Again, reg. 4 forbids people who are attending vehicles conveying petrol to smoke, or to carry matches and lighters. Regulation 5 then adds to the picture by providing that nothing capable of igniting inflammable vapour should be allowed on any vehicle conveying

---

[3]They appear as S.I. 1957 No. 191. Further, it should be noticed that they are slightly amended by the Petroleum-Spirit (Conveyance by Road) Regulations 1958 (S.I. 1958 No. 962).
[4]The vessels can be of a capacity not exceeding 10 gallons if they are metal, but otherwise they must not be of a capacity which exceeds 2 gallons.

petrol, and reg. 6 completes it by requiring vehicles which convey petrol to carry efficient fire extinguishers.

Part 2 of the regulations, as was explained earlier, deals exclusively with the conveyance of petrol by road in tank wagons or tank trailers. It contains a number of detailed regulations which space does not permit to be included, but reference to two of them will indicate the intensity of the approach. Thus, the first concern is with the construction and maintenance of the wagon or trailer. From reg. 11 (and from the First Schedule to which reg. 11 refers),[5] we learn that wagons and trailers shall be constructed strongly and of fire-resistant materials. Moreover, while the capacity of a tank wagon may not in any case exceed four thousand gallons, and only in certain instances exceed one thousand five hundred gallons, the capacity of a tank trailer may not exceed one thousand gallons. Passing on then to reg. 15 we find that during the filling or emptying of a wagon or trailer, the vehicle must be constantly attended by a competent person, and he must make sure that, amongst other things, the engine of the vehicle is stopped throughout the operation, and is not run again until the tank and the storage tank have been securely closed.

Part 3, in conclusion, is concerned, as was mentioned earlier, with the conveyance of petrol by road in vehicles other than tank wagons or tank trailers, and in this part we must focus our attention on regs. 22, 23 and 24.

Regulation 22 relates to the vehicle itself, and requires it to possess sides and back, to be of strong construction, and to be maintained in good order.[6] Regulation 23, on the other hand, has regard to the vessels in which the petrol is contained. *Either* a vessel must be made of metal, securely closed, in good order, and able to hold not more than fifty[7] gallons of petrol, *or else* it must be made of glass or other suitable material, securely closed, able to hold not more than one pint of petrol, and packed in sawdust,

---

[5]This Schedule contains numerous provisions as to construction; and reg. 11 requires tank wagons and trailers to comply with those provisions.

[6]In addition, it must comply with some of the provisions contained in the First Schedule.

[7]Where certain mixtures of petrol are involved, then the figure is ninety, not fifty, gallons.

or similar material, inside a strong outer container.[8] Finally, reg. 24 provides that loads of petrol being conveyed by road shall be protected from fire by a cover of fire-resisting material.

So much then, for the regulations governing the conveyance of petrol by road. Still, however, the picture as regards inflammable liquids is not complete, and we must continue further:

If one looks at s. 19 of the Petroleum (Consolidation) Act 1928, one will find that power is given to the Queen to apply (by Order in Council) any of the provisions of the 1928 Act *to any substance*, and advantage has been taken of this power to bring under control the handling and use of many dangerous liquids. In this context, then, let us consider,

(xvi) *The Petroleum (Inflammable Liquids) Order* 1968[9]

By this Order, a number of sections of the 1928 Act have been applied to a very long list of inflammable liquids.[10] Amongst the most important of the sections so applied is s. 6. This section, as mentioned previously, gives the Secretary of State power to make regulations as to the conveyance of petrol by road, and the order enables the Secretary of State to do the same with regard to the inflammable liquids given in the list. In fact, such regulations have been speedily made, and are known as the Inflammable Liquids (Conveyance by Road) Regulations 1968.[11]

Our treatment of the legislation and delegated legislation which governs the handling and use of petrol and other inflammable liquids, has been somewhat lengthy, and in this respect a comparison can be drawn with the treatment given to the regulation of cinemas. Wherever there appears a high degree of fire risk, the control exerted has, of necessity, to be precise and detailed, and accordingly it does not lend itself to brief consideration.

Such, then, are amongst the more important of the many and varied enactments which, until recently, composed our law on fire precautions. Now, though, we have to consider the Fire

---

[8]Notice also that this outer container must not contain more than three gallons of petrol altogether, it must be securely closed, and capable of withstanding the ordinary risks of handling and transport.
[9]This Order appears as S.I. 1968 No. 570.
[10]They are set out in a Schedule to the order.
[11]They appear as S.I. 1968 No. 927.

Precautions Act 1971, and before dealing with its content, to make a few, preliminary observations.

First, a contrast must be drawn between this Act and those to which attention has already been paid. This is an Act completely and exclusively directed to fire precautions, whereas in the other Acts to which reference has been made fire precautions constituted merely one of a number of issues, and in studying those Acts it was a question simply of selecting for investigation in each case the relevant sections.

Secondly, throughout our consideration of the Fire Precautions Act, we must constantly keep in mind that it is not immediately operative. Section 44(3) provides:

"This Act shall come into operation on such day as the Secretary of State[12] may by order made by statutory instrument appoint, and different dates may be appointed . . . for different purposes."

Thus, it is an Act which, over a period of years, can be gradually brought into operation by successive pieces of delegated legislation, and necessarily so, for such is its nature and scope that its immediate operation would not be feasible.[13]

Thirdly, notice must be given to the fact that as certain of its portions become operative, so they will take the place of earlier legislation concerned with the same issues, and this means that parts of the legislation to which attention has already been paid will one day become obsolete.

Finally, as the reader may be well aware, the Act is both lengthy and complex, and it must be emphasised that what follows is but an outline survey of its principal features.

So, with these points in the background, let us proceed to the substance of the Act:

Section 1 provides that a "fire certificate" (issued by a fire authority) shall be compulsory for premises which are put to certain uses,[14] and, for this purpose enables the Secretary of State

---

[12]In this instance, the Home Secretary.

[13]In technical language it is an "enabling Act", i.e., it enables the Home Office to bring various parts into operation as and when it deems suitable.

[14]It is noteworthy that in the Fire Precautions Act emphasis is placed on the use to which premises are put, rather than on the persons using them. This should obviate the difficulty sometimes encountered in exercising control over premises not used by members of the "public" (used, for instance, only by members of associations or societies).

(i.e., the Home Secretary) to "designate" uses. He may only, however, designate a use if it comes within the following classes of uses: use for any purpose involving sleeping accommodation; use as an institution providing treatment or care; use for entertainment, recreation or instruction, or for the purposes of any club or society; use for purposes of teaching, training or research; and use for any purpose involving access to the premises by the public.

The scope afforded the Home Secretary is therefore extensive, but in s. 2 one finds a list of excepted premises, i.e., of premises for which no fire certificate shall be required under s. 1, and these include factories, offices, shops and railway premises, places used for religious worship, and premises occupied as a single, private dwelling.

In contrast with the wide impact of s. 1, s. 3 is aimed at a more particular problem: namely the risk of fire in flats and maisonettes. In more detail, the section is concerned with premises which are used or to be used as a dwelling, and which, *inter alia*, have living accommodation below the ground floor, two or more floors above the ground floor, or in which the living accommodation has a floor six metres or more above ground level. If the fire authority is of the opinion that any premises come within the section, it may, at its discretion, serve a notice on the owner, occupier or manager of the premises, stating that upon the coming into force of the notice, a fire certificate will be required. Section 3(2), however, excludes from the impact of the section certain premises: thus, any premises occupied as a single, private dwelling are excluded, and likewise, any houses in multiple occupation.[15]

Before proceeding further, mention must be made of the fact that there is a basic, if not immediately apparent, difference between s. 1 and s. 3. Under s. 1, when orders are made requiring fire certificates to be obtained for premises put to certain uses, it will be necessary for applications to be made to the fire authorities for such certificates. In contrast with this situation, when s. 3 is made operative, it is the fire authorities themselves who may notify owners, occupiers or managers of flats and

---

[15]Note the control exercised over multiple occupancies by the Housing Act 1961 and the Housing Regulations 1961.

maisonettes that fire certificates will be required.

Turning next to s. 5 one sees that when an application for a fire certificate is made, the fire authority must carry out an inspection of the premises. If, having carried out an inspection, the authority is satisfied that (a) the means of escape, (b) the means provided for securing the safe and effective use of the means of escape, (c) the means for fighting fire provided for use by persons in the building, and (d) the means for giving persons in the premises warning in case of fire, are such as may reasonably be required in the circumstances, it shall issue a certificate. Should the authority not be satisfied on the other hand, it must inform the applicant of the steps he must take to satisfy the authority, and notify him that a certificate will not be issued unless those steps are taken.

Continuing further to s. 6, one meets a section concerned with the contents of a fire certificate. In particular, s. 6(1) provides that every fire certificate shall specify: (a) the use or uses which the certificate covers; (b) the means of escape with which the premises are provided; (c) the means provided for securing the safe and effective use of the means of escape; (d) the type, number and location of the means for fighting fire provided in the building for use by persons therein; and (e) the type, number and location of the means of giving warning in case of fire to persons in the premises. Again, s. 6(2) provides that the fire authority may impose, by means of the fire certificate, such requirements as are considered appropriate (a) for securing that the means of escape are properly maintained and kept free from obstruction; (b) for securing that the means with which the building is provided as mentioned in s. 6(1)(c) to (e) are properly maintained; (c) for securing that persons employed in the premises receive appropriate instruction in what to do in case of fire; (d) for limiting the number of persons permissibly present at any one time; and (e) as to other precautions to be observed.

Section 7 puts teeth into the Act by creating offences in relation to the provisions which have gone before. Thus, for example, under s. 7(1) if premises are put to a "designated" use and require a fire certificate under s. 1, should no certificate be in force covering that use, the occupier of the premises will be guilty of an offence. And again, for instance, under s. 7(2), if any premises are used as a dwelling at any time while s. 3 applies to them and a notice is in force, then should there not be a fire certificate in force in respect of those premises, the notified person will be guilty of an offence.[16] Mention should be made of the fact, though, s. 9 makes available a system of appeals for those aggrieved by matters arising in connection with fire certificates.[17]

A change of conditions in the physical sense may obviously have great affect upon premises from the fire precautions point of view, and full recognition is afforded to this problem by s. 8.

Section 8(1) empowers a fire authority (so long as a fire certificate is in force with respect to the premises) to have a building inspected for the purpose of ascertaining whether there has been a change of conditions by reason of which any matters mentioned in s. 6 (1)(b) to (e) have become inadequate, and s. 8(2) provides that if (while a fire certificate is in force with respect to any premises) it is proposed, *inter alia*, to make a material, structural alteration to the premises or a material alteration in the internal arrangement of the premises or its furniture, the occupier shall give notice of the proposals to the fire authority. It is then provided under s. 8(4) that if the fire authority is satisfied that the carrying out of the proposals would result in any of the matters mentioned in s. 6(1)(b) to (e) becoming inadequate, it may inform the occupier of steps which would have to be taken to prevent this happening, and, if those steps are taken, must amend the certificate or issue a new one.

Like s. 7, s. 10 gives the Act "bite", for it provides that if in the case of (a), any premises which are or are to be put to a use mentioned in s. 1(2),[18] and (b) any premises to which s. 3 applies, the fire authority is satisfied that the fire risk is so serious the use of the premises ought to be prohibited or restricted, it can complain to the court. Then, the court, if similarly satisfied, can prohibit or restrict the use of the premises until such steps have been taken as, in the opinion of the court, are necessary to reduce the risk to a reasonable level.

Turning next to s. 11, one finds a section designed to repair

---

[16]He will not be guilty if he shows he no longer occupied the specified position.
[17]Regarding appeals see also s. 4.
[18]Whether or not designated by the Home Secretary. Note, though, that s. 10 does not apply to premises which fall in s. 2.

a strange omission. Unlike Scotland, in this country, that part of the Building Regulations which is devoted to fire precautions does not include any requirements as to the provision of means of escape. Accordingly, s. 11(1) provides that "the power of the Secretary of State under s. 4 of the Public Health Act 1961 to make building regulations . . . shall include power to impose requirements as to the provision of means of escape from buildings in case of fire and means . . . for securing that such means of escape can be safely and effectively used at all material times".[19]

Passing on from s. 11 to s. 12 one sees power being given to the Secretary of State to make regulations about fire precautions. Thus s. 12(1) says that in the case of any use of premises which can be designated under s. 1, the Secretary may by regulations make provision as to the precautions which, as regards premises put to that use, are to be taken in relation to the risk to persons in case of fire[20]. And again, s. 12(2) provides that regulations may be similarly made regarding premises which, while s. 3 applies to them and a notice is in force in relation to them, are used as a dwelling. Moreover, s. 12(3) goes on to say that without in any way prejudicing the generality of the powers conferred upon the Secretary, regulations made by him may in particular impose requirements, *inter alia*, (a) as to the provision, maintenance and keeping free from obstruction of means of escape; (b) as to the provision and maintenance of means for securing the safe and effective use of means of escape; (c) as to the provision and maintenance of means for fighting fire and giving warning in case of fire; (d) as to the internal construction of the premises and materials used in construction; (e) for prohibiting the use of furniture or equipment of any specified description; and (f) for securing that persons employed to work in the premises receive instruction in what to do in case of fire.

With regard to the enforcement of the Act, reference must be made to ss. 18, 19 and 20. Section 18 provides that it shall be the duty of every fire authority to enforce the Act in their area, and

---

[19]Such regulations are in preparation.
[20]Nothing in any regulations so made, however, shall apply to premises falling in s. 2 with the exception of premises used for religious worship.

to appoint inspectors for that purpose; s. 19 provides that fire inspectors and inspectors appointed under s. 18 may do anything necessary for the purpose of carrying the Act into effect (and in particular bestows upon such persons remarkably wide powers of entry, inquiry and inspection); and s. 20 empowers officers of fire brigades to exercise the powers given by s. 19 to fire inspectors on their behalf.

Finally, reference must be made once more to the already-mentioned fact that as, gradually, the Act is rendered operative, and its provisions carried into effect, so some of the earlier legislation will eventually be replaced. Thus, for instance, s. 30(1) provides that where building regulations imposing requirements as to the provision of means of escape in case of fire are applicable to a proposed building, neither s. 59(1) nor s. 60 of the Public Health Act 1936, will impinge.[1] Again, s. 30(3) provides that with regard to any premises in respect of which a fire certificate is in force, or to which a notice under s. 3 relates, or to which any regulations made under s. 12 apply, neither s. 59, sub-ss (2) to (4)[2] nor s. 60 of the Public Health Act 1936, will be applicable. In a similar context, s. 31 of the Act is also of interest. Section 31(1) provides that where any enactment provides for the licensing of premises, and the licensing authority is required or authorised to impose terms, conditions or restrictions, then in the case of any such premises, so long as a fire certificate is in force, any term, condition or restriction shall be of no effect in so far as it concerns any matter regarding which requirements are or could be imposed by the certificate. As has been explained, control regarding

---

[1]Section 59(1) provides that where plans of a building are deposited with a local authority, and the section applies to the particular building, the local authority shall reject the plans unless the building is shown to be provided with satisfactory means of ingress and egress. The section applies to places including theatres, halls, shops, restaurants and schools. Section 60, which applies to high buildings let out as flats, or used for such purposes as hotels, inns, boarding schools, etc., imposes a duty on the local authority, where it appears that an existing or proposed building will not be provided with proper means of escape, to require the necessary work to be carried out.

[2]As noted above, s. 59 applies to theatres, halls, restaurants, etc. Section 59(2) states that where it appears to a local authority that a building to which the section applies does not have satisfactory means of ingress and egress, the authority can require the owner to make proper provision; s. 59(3) enables the court to restrict the use of a building if the authority believes immediate action to be necessary; and s. 59(4) requires means of ingress and egress to be kept free from obstruction while persons are assembled.

fire precautions is exercised in many spheres by means of the licensing system. Before leaving this aspect of the Act, special mention should be made perhaps of the Cinematograph Regulations. Section 12(11) provides that once s. 12 has come into operation, it will no longer be possible to make regulations by virtue of s. 2(1)(*a*) of the Cinematograph Act 1952, under the Cinematograph Act 1909, but any regulations which are in force at the relevant point in time will have effect as if they had been made under this section.

CONCLUSION

In conclusion, it must be said that while the way in which the law relating to fire precautions has grown makes it a difficult subject to study, it is at the moment at a most interesting stage of development. Until the Fire Precautions Act is rendered operational, only premises falling under the Factories Act and the Offices, Shops and Railway Premises Act are subject to control by the system of issuing "fire certificates", a system generally considered to be by far the most suitable. By applying the certification process to a very wide class of premises, the Act will gradually achieve a most welcome measure of rationalisation.

Such is the span of the Act, that it will be a long time before it becomes completely effective, and one would assume that inasmuch as the Home Office is concerned with the task of bringing the Act into force step by step, its members have established an order of priorities. In view of the present alarm over outbreaks of fire in hotels, for instance, such premises would appear to warrant expeditious treatment.

It is not only, however, the implementation of the Fire Precautions Act which will slowly expand and improve this area of the law, for the Department of Employment and Productivity is in the midst of preparing a comprehensive revision of the Factories Act and the Offices, Shops and Railway Premises Act, and, with regard to precautions against fire, their object will be to rationalise the law, strengthen it, and render it more effective.

[N.B. There is, in Appendix I, a brief note on some protections afforded to individual consumers. Since this book went to press. significant events concerning the Fire Precautions Act have taken place, and are explained separately in the addenda on p. 93.]

Chapter 4

LIABILITY FOR DAMAGE CAUSED BY FIRE

INTRODUCTION

So far, we have considered the legal position of the fire service, and the impact of the fire prevention legislation, but we have not as yet considered the question of liability for damage caused by fire. In order to do this, we must turn to the common law, because it is the common law which has gradually developed the principles governing liability for damage so caused. Part of the "law of tort", it is not a very large area of law, but it enjoys a long and ancient history. The earliest case is to be found at the beginning of the fifteenth century,[1] and the principles have gradually evolved during the supervening period.

DEVELOPMENT OF PRINCIPLES

The main question with which the mediaeval judges were concerned was a simple one: if X lights a fire on his property, and the fire spreads to Y's property, causing damage to Y or his goods, is X liable to compensate Y? It remains still the most important question in the field, the answer to which is as vital in the twentieth century as in the fifteenth, for it involves the basis and extent of legal responsibility for fire.

Legal historians tell us that they are unable to discover what precisely was the attitude of the judges to this question from the

---

[1] *Beaulieu* v. *Finglam* (1401), Y.B. 2 Hen. 4, f. 18, pl. 6.

fifteenth to the eighteenth century. Clearly, there were two possibilities. Either, (1) X was absolutely liable for any damage which his fire caused to Y or Y's property, or, (2) X was only liable for damage so caused, if, in regard to his fire, he had acted carelessly. If the first rule were operative, then X lit his fire "at his peril"; in lawyers' language it was a case of *strict liability*. If, however, the second rule were operative, then X was only liable for *negligence*, a rule which appears more reasonable.

The difficulty is that some cases supported the former rule, and some the latter, and which of the two rules was correct seems never to have been established. For instance, in *Turberville* v. *Stampe*,[2] HOLT, C.J., appears to take the line that X would be liable to Y only if he were negligent, while in the fairly recent case of *Collingwood* v. *Home and Colonial Stores, Ltd.*,[3] Lord WRIGHT spoke of the early common law attitude in this way:

" ... if a fire spread from a man's premises and did damage to adjoining premises, he was liable ... on the broad ground that it was his duty at his own peril to keep any fire that originated on his premises from spreading to and damaging his neighbour's premises."[4]

It seems, though, that by the end of the seventeenth century most lawyers thought that the former rule was the correct one, and that X was absolutely liable to compensate Y if his fire spread to Y's premises and caused damage: whether or not Y had been careless did not matter. Again, it seems that the lawyers thought so harsh a rule to be unfair, and in 1707 an Act was passed to mitigate its harshness. This Act provided that no action should be brought against a person in whose house a fire should accidentally begin, a rule which was repeated in s. 86 of the Fires Prevention (Metropolis) Act 1774 in the following words:

"No action ... shall be ... maintained ... against any person in whose house ... or other building ... or on whose estate any fire shall ... accidentally begin, nor shall any recompense be made by such person for any damage suffered thereby ..."

There are a number of matters arising from this section which

[2](1967), 1 Ld. Raym 264.
[3][1936] 3 All E.R. 200.
[4]*Ibid.*, at p. 203.

we must consider, but before we turn to them a point of basic importance must be borne in mind: Although the Act is entitled the Fires Prevention (Metropolis) Act, it does not apply only in London. On the contrary, it extends throughout the country.

Turning then to the various matters which arise from s. 86, we must first consider exactly what is meant by " . . . any fire shall . . . accidentally begin, . . ." With regard to the words "any fire", we learn from *Salmond on Torts*[5] that they must cover fires which are intentionally lit, but which then accidentally spread from the premises of source. Obviously the words cannot just refer to fires caused by lightning or spontaneous combustion.

What, though, of the word "accidentally", the most vital word in the section? This is generally taken to mean, as was held in *Filliter* v. *Phippard*,[6] "*without negligence*". Accordingly, if a man acts with care he obtains the protection of the Act, and no action can be brought against him, but if he is negligent, the Act does not help him and he is liable. Lord WRIGHT in *Collingwood* v. *Home and Colonial Stores, Ltd.*,[7] you will recall, thought that at Common Law a man was *absolutely* liable if his fire spread and caused damage, and he concluded that the Act changed the common law rule. Again, in *Mulholland & Tedd, Ltd.* v. *Baker*[8] ASQUITH, J., pointed out that at common law a person was liable for the escape of his fire regardless of any care he might have taken, but that since 1774 he is liable only if he has been negligent. In this particular case the plaintiff and the defendant owned adjoining shops. The defendant lit some paper close to some paraffin which he had stored on his premises, and the fire which ensued spread to the plaintiff's property. The judge found that the defendant had been negligent, and that the Act did not therefore protect him.

Thus, since the passing of the 1774 Act, it has gradually become clear that a person who negligently causes a fire to begin on his premises is liable if it spreads to his neighbour's premises. If he is not negligent, however, the Act saves him from liability.

But this is by no means the end of the matter. A further question

---

[5] 15th Edn., at p. 427.
[6] (1847), 11 Q.B. 347.
[7] [1936] 3 All E.R. 200, at p. 203.
[8] [1939] 3 All E.R. 253.

has been raised as to what happens where a fire is started without any negligence, but is negligently allowed to spread, and in its spreading causes damage.[9] From *Musgrove* v. *Pandelis*[10] we gather that in such a situation the Act provides no protection to the defendant, and he is obliged to compensate the plaintiff for the loss suffered.

INTERESTING

Case.

In somewhat similar vein is the Australian case of *Goldman* v. *Hargrave*,[11] which was decided only a few years ago. In this case a tall "red gum" tree on D's land was struck by lightning, and began to burn. The following day, D had the tree felled, which was the proper course to take, but then, rather than extinguishing the fire with water as he should have done, he decided to let the tree burn itself out. He could reasonably have foreseen that the fire might revive, yet took no steps to prevent it from so doing. A day or two later it revived dramatically, spread to P's land, and caused considerable damage. The Judicial Committee of the Privy Council[12] held that D was negligent, and further, that the Act of 1774 provided him with no protection, because the damage had been caused by the fire which had negligently been allowed to "revive", *and not by the fire which had accidentally begun.*

In both this case and the preceding case the person is not made liable on account of the fire which accidentally began, but on account of the fire which he negligently permitted to increase.

So far, we have spoken only of the situation where an occupier of premises lights a fire which spreads to other premises, and causes damage. We have not as yet considered the position where a fire is started on premises *by some other person other than the occupier of the premises.* In this event, if the fire spreads and causes damage, can the occupier of the premises be held liable? The answer appears to be "yes", if (*a*) the person lighting the fire is in some way under control of the occupier, and (*b*) that same person is negligent. Persons whom the law would consider to

---

[9] Of general interest in this sphere is the "stubble field fire". Every harvest time farmers deliberately burn off their stubble fields, and fire brigades receive numerous calls to deal with fires as a result of the "controlled burning" becoming uncontrolled and spreading to nearby property.

[10] [1919] 2 K.B. 43.

[11] [1966] 2 All E.R. 989 (P.C.).

[12] This is a committee composed of judges of the House of Lords, and one which acts as an ultimate "court of appeal" for Commonwealth cases.

be "under the control" of the occupier, would include his guests, his servants, or persons who come on to his premises to carry out some specific task.[13] If persons such as these act negligently, and in so doing cause damage by fire, they can make the occupier liable to compensate the one who suffers.

The idea that an occupier of premises could be held liable in this way is a very old one. If we turn to *Beaulieu* v. *Finglam*[14] at the beginning of the fifteenth century, we find Markham, J., saying that a man is liable for each person who enters his house by his leave or knowledge if he does any act "with a candle or aught else whereby his neighbour's house is burnt".[15]

Moreover, one should notice that far back in 1401 the notion of "control" was present. The occupier was responsible for the person who entered his house "by his leave or knowledge". In other words, he was responsible for the person over whom he could exercise control. Even at this early stage of development the common law was able to distinguish between persons over whom the occupier could exercise control and those over whom he could not. Thus, no liability would be imposed on the occupier for damage caused by fire which originated from the act of a stranger, or, for that matter, from an act of God. Not only is the idea of long standing, it has remained unchanged through the centuries. For instance, in *Filliter* v. *Phippard*[16] in the middle of the nineteenth century, it was said that where damage is caused by fire due to the negligence of the defendant *or his servants*, the defendant is liable. And again, only a few years ago in *Balfour* v. *Barty-King*[17] we find an occupier being held responsible

[13] I.e., "independent contractors".
[14] (1401), Y.B. 2 Hen. 4, f. 18, pl. 6.
[15] See Fifoot, *History and Sources of the Common Law, Tort and Contract*, p. 167.
[16] (1847), 11 Q.B. 347.
[17] [1957] 1 Q.B. 496, C.A. And yet again, to similar effect, is the very recent case of *H. & N., Emanuel Ltd* v. *Greater London Council*, [1971] 2 All E.R. 835, C.A. Here, the council were held liable for damage caused by sparks flying on to neighbouring property from a bonfire lit by the workmen of an independent contractor engaged on the demolition of some council bungalows. The Court of Appeal held that the occupier of premises is liable for the escape of fire caused not only by the negligence of his servant, but also of his independent contractor and of anyone else on his land with his permission. He would not be liable, however, for the escape of fire caused by negligence when the negligence was that of a stranger. In this instance, such was not the case. The council had a sufficient degree of control over the activities of people on the premises, and could reasonably have anticipated that the men would light a fire.

for the damage resulting from a spread of fire caused by the negligence of his independent contractor

It must always be kept in mind, though, when considering the liability of the occupier for the acts of others, that he is only held responsible if those acts are negligent, and if they are performed by persons who are under his control.

In all the material so far considered, we have been focusing our attention on the person *who may be sued*. We must pay attention also, though, to the person *who may sue*. In other words, we must turn for a moment from defendants to plaintiffs. Up to this point our plaintiffs have been the occupiers of premises to which fire has spread, and who have in some way suffered loss or damage. But the right to bring an action is by no means restricted to such persons; it is not only the "adjoining occupiers" who can sue. If fire spreads from X's premises to Y's, and damages Z's tractor which is standing temporarily on Y's premises, Z can sue X. The right to sue is not limited to the occupier of the premises to which the fire spreads, but extends to any person whose property is injured.

From dealing with liability for damage *directly* caused by fire, we must pass on to a consideration of damage *indirectly* so caused. In this sphere, a number of different problems arise, and we must look at them in turn:

First, what is the attitude of the law towards people who perform acts with the object of extinguishing a fire, and thereby avoiding damage to persons or property, if, in performing those acts, they cause damage to other property? If the people who perform such acts are sued by the owners of the damaged property, can they successfully defend themselves by pleading that the danger of the fire rendered their acts necessary?

In this instance, the answer *appears* to be that where persons or property are in real and imminent danger, a man may cause damage to other property, and justify his acts by reference to their necessity. In the case of *Dewey* v. *White*[18] for example, in the early years of the last century, a stack of chimneys belonging to a house was threatened by fire and in danger of falling on to a road. Because of the danger, a fireman threw the stack down, and in so

---

[18](1827), Mood & M. 56.

doing damaged an adjoining house belonging to a third person. When sued by that person for the damage caused, the fireman successfully pleaded the defence of "necessity".[19]

It seems, however, that to support a defence of necessity the acts done must be *reasonably necessary*; i.e., they must be acts *a reasonable man* would perform. This we learn from *Cope* v. *Sharpe*[20] in 1912, as also the important point that in deciding whether or not the acts done were "reasonably necessary", the situation must be considered at the moment of interference, *not after the event*. In other words, the question is whether or not a reasonable man in the emergency which arose would have considered the acts reasonably necessary, and not whether as things turned out the acts were *in fact* reasonably necessary. Such a distinction is obviously fair, and vital!

Again, an important facet of the defence of necessity is its scope. It is not a defence which only avails a member of a fire brigade: *any* individual may raise it.

In the field of damage indirectly caused by fire, a second problem which requires discussion is that of the fireman who is injured in the course of his duties. It sometimes happens that fire authorities act negligently, and so cause the injury of a fireman whom they employ, or again, that occupiers of premises in which fire breaks out act negligently, and so occasion the suffering of a fireman engaged in fighting the fire. In circumstances such as these, it is necessary to consider how a fireman will fare, who, seeking compensation for the damage done to him, brings an action for negligence against the fire authority which employs him, or the occupiers of premises in which he fights a fire.

Generally speaking, his task is not an easy one, because it is "up hill" work for a plaintiff to prove that a defendant has been negligent. To succeed, he has to show that in the circumstances the defendant owed him a duty to take care, that he broke that duty, and that in consequence damage was occasioned. Cases which are brought by reason of negligent acts and omissions

---

[19] A note here is in point, regarding s.30 of the Fire Services Act 1947. Were the defence of necessity of a more certain character, the provisions of s. 30 could be considered superfluous.

[20] *Cope* v. *Sharpe* (*No. 2*), [1912] 1 K.B. 496, C.A.

cover an immense variety of incidents, but in *Watt* v. *Hertfordshire County Council*[1] there is an instance involving a member of a fire brigade.

In this case a fireman was injured by a heavy jack which had been placed in a lorry conveying him to the scene of an accident. He took the view that his employer, the local fire authority, was negligent in requiring him to travel in a vehicle containing so dangerous an object, and accordingly he brought an action. In the event, however, his action failed, the Court of Appeal holding that the fire authority was not guilty of negligence. In so holding, the court was clearly influenced by the special nature of the service and the inevitably hazardous character of its activities, for the point was made that an ordinary commercial employer might well have been held to have broken the duty of care which he owed to his employees had he required them to ride in a vehicle conveying an object of that kind. Thus, Lord SINGLETON said: "The fire service is a service which must always involve risk for those employed in it . . .";[2] while Lord DENNING remarked that " . . . the saving of life or limb justifies taking considerable risks, and . . . there have never been wanting in this country men ready to take those risks, notably in the fire service."[3]

Again, in seeking to bring an action for negligence, the injured fireman may find his path to success blocked by a defence known as *volenti non fit injuria*. This is a defence which runs through a large area of the law of tort, and means quite simply "to the willing is not done injury". In other words, the defendant who raises this defence is saying to the plaintiff: "In the circumstances, you know there was a risk that you might be injured, but you accepted that risk in the sense that, when you acted, you implicitly agreed to forego any compensation should injury occur. In effect, you precluded yourself from bringing an action in respect of the injury you have suffered." It is a defence which is used, for example, against people who participate in games or sports, or against people who consent to undergo an operation, and,

[1][1954] 2 All E.R. 368.
[2]*Ibid.*, at p. 369.
[3]*Ibid.*, at p. 371.

64

so far as firemen are concerned it is possible for it to be raised with success because they have elected to follow a dangerous calling. Thus, they may be taken by the court to be aware of and to have accepted the risks which are inherent in their hazardous way of life. Notice, though, that I only say "may be". The court will not necessarily take this view, for all depends on the facts involved in the particular case in issue.

To see the defence of *volenti non fit injuria* at work in this sphere we must look at the case of *Merrington* v. *Ironbridge Metal Works*[4] in 1952. In this case a fire broke out in a factory in which manufacturing processes were carried on in such a way as to create an exceptional and unnecessary risk of fire and explosions. A fireman who was fighting the fire was injured, and, believing that it was the negligence of the owners of the factory which caused his injury, brought an action against them. In their defence, the owners pleaded *volenti non fit injuria*.

The court held in favour of the fireman. The view was taken that the owners of the factory owed persons in the position of the fireman a duty to keep the factory free from exceptional and unnecessary danger, and that, in breaking the duty, they had acted negligently. Further, the court held that the fireman was not willing to accept the risk of such injury, because he did not appreciate the hazardous character of the conditions brought about by the defendants' carelessness, and did not agree to assume the risk without compensation. Moreover, the judge was of the opinion that the fireman was acting under the compulsion of duty, and was not therefore in a position to make a free choice as to whether or not he would accept a risk.

In this particular case, therefore, the defence of *volenti non fit injuria* failed, and the defendants were made to compensate the fireman for the injury which they negligently caused him. It may well be, though, that in different circumstances, the defence of *volenti* could be used successfully to defeat a fireman's claim.

The third and final problem in the field of damage *indirectly* caused by fire, raises for discussion the converse of the problem just considered. In contrast with the situation where a fireman *is injured* in the course of his duties, one has now to look at the

---

[4] [1952] 2 All E.R. 1101.

situation where a fireman in the course of his duties himself *causes injury*, whether that injury be to persons or property. To put it simply, what is the position if a fireman acts negligently and causes damage?

For the person who is injured or whose property is damaged by reason of a fireman's negligence, there is usually not much to be gained from suing the fireman. Generally speaking, the ordinary fireman is not a man of great financial means, and it is not worth while to bring an action against him. It is, however, far more in the interests of the aggrieved person to bring an action against the *employer* of the fireman, namely, the relevant fire authority. If the aggrieved person takes that course, he will be utilising the concept of "vicarious liability", by which is meant the liability of one person on behalf of another. It is a concept which operates to make an employer liable when his employee, acting in the course of his employment, negligently causes harm to a third person or to a third person's property. In this instance, the person who suffers the harm would be saying to the fire authority, "a fireman acting in the course of his duties has negligently caused me harm; you are the employers of that fireman and I hold you responsible for his negligence". The question then remains, can this concept be successfully raised? In other words, can a fire authority be made vicariously liable for a fireman who, in the course of his employment with that authority, negligently causes harm to persons or property? From a number of cases in which the question has been raised, the answer is clearly "yes".[5]

CONCLUSION

In this chapter we have considered, from the point of view of legal responsibility, a number of situations in which damage is caused, either directly or indirectly, by the spreading of fire. As has been seen, the principles governing that responsibility have developed through the centuries, emerging gradually from the decisions reached by the judges. In the cases brought

---

[5]See, for instance, *Ward* v. *London County Council*, [1938] 2 All E.R. 341;
Joyce v. *Metropolitan Board of Works* (1881), 44 L.T. 811;
Kilboy v. *South Eastern Fire Area Joint Area Committee*, 1952 S.C. 280.

before the courts involving injury or damage caused by fire, the questions raised are those which run throughout the whole law of private injuries; questions such as: On what grounds should a person be held liable for the damage occasioned? To what extent should a person be held liable for the damage caused? What defences can a person raise to justify or excuse his acts or omissions? In this particular sphere, however, they are questions which can prove exceptionally difficult to answer. Not long ago it was said in the House of Lords that "Words are . . . volatile . . . They travel fast and far afield."[6] It was a comment which could equally well have been made about fire.

---

[6] *Per* Lord PEARCE in *Hedley Byrne & Co., Ltd.* v. *Heller & Partners, Ltd.*, [1964] A.C. 465 H.L., at p. 534.

Chapter 5

FIRE INSURANCE

INTRODUCTION

In this chapter we shall be concerned exclusively with the practice of insuring property against the risk of damage or destruction by fire. It is, of course, a very common practice and an old one. Over the years, it has gradually become governed by a fairly large and complicated set of legal rules, to the principal ones of which we must now devote our attention.

The first point to notice is that the man who seeks to insure his property against the risk of fire, must enter for this purpose into an agreement (or, to use the technical word, a "contract"). In so doing, he agrees to pay what is known as a "premium", to an insurance company or to a Lloyd's underwriter (as the case may be), who, in return, undertakes to make payment in the event of the property being damaged or destroyed by fire. Now the law of fire insurance is made up of rules which are designed to govern contracts of this nature, and also to establish the legal positions of the people who enter into them. Before we look at the rules though, we must bear in mind the names by which lawyers refer to those who participate in contracts of fire insurance: the person who has his property insured is known as "the assured", and the people who run the company which insures the property are known as the "insurers".

So much then for the background, now let us turn to the principles of law.

THE LEGAL PRINCIPLES

(i) *The contract*

To the question "what is a contract of insurance?", the lawyer's answer is this: A contract of insurance is one in which the insurers pay a sum of money on the happening of a specified event, and it is legally essential that the happening of the event should be uncertain; uncertain that is, either in the sense that it is uncertain *as to whether it will happen or not*, or else in the sense that it is uncertain *as to when it will happen*.

Again, while dealing with fundamental matters, it should be noticed that the law requires a person to have what is called "an insurable interest" in the property which he seeks to have insured. The value or the extent of his interest in the property does not matter; all that matters is that its damage or destruction would cause him loss. So, for instance, he need not *own* the property he wants insured. A tenant has an insurable interest in the property which he enjoys. Equally, he need not physically possess the property he wants insured. A creditor whose debt is secured by a mortgage on some property has an insurable interest in that property. In both cases, were fire to occasion the damage or destruction of the property, it would be to the disadvantage of the person who seeks to have it insured.

Having established these fundamental matters, we must next consider the chief feature of contracts of insurance, a feature which in lawyers' language, would be expressed in this way: "Contracts of insurance are contracts of the utmost good faith." Now what exactly does that mean? It means that the parties to the contract must act with the utmost good faith in the sense that the common law imposes upon them a duty to make a full and candid disclosure of all material facts. It is a duty the full force of which impinges most noticeably on the would be assured. The insurers ask him detailed and specific questions about every fact which is material to his proposal for insurance, and it is in answering them that his "utmost good faith" is exercised. He must neither fail to disclose a material fact nor misrepresent a material fact, a state of affairs which leads one to ask, what are "material facts"?

Any fact is material which would influence the judgment of

a prudent insurer in fixing the premium, or determining whether he will take the risk. For example, if at the time of insuring certain premises a fire has just been extinguished in the adjoining premises, and is imminently likely to break out again, such a circumstance would clearly constitute a "material fact".[1] And similarly, if it is sought to insure premises against fire, the insurer may consider it most material to ascertain whether the person seeking the insurance has sustained previous losses to premises by fire.[2]

What happens, then, if one party to the contract can show that the other party has failed to disclose or has misrepresented a material fact? The answer, very simply, is that the party who is able to establish such a failure or misrepresentation can avoid (i.e., "get out of") the contract. Furthermore, this is still the case, *even though a misrepresentation is innocently and honestly made.*

While considering the requirement of "utmost good faith" it should be emphasised that it is a requirement of the common law, and applies generally to contracts of fire insurance. It is quite in order, though, for the parties to a particular contract to agree that the requirement shall be in some way extended or restricted. Thus, it may be extended so as to include the giving of particulars of facts not normally taken to be material, or restricted so as to deny the right of avoiding the contract where a misrepresentation is innocently and honestly made.

In contrast with the deep interest which the law takes in the good faith of the parties, it evinces no interest in the degree of formality which they choose to attach to their agreement. There is no legal requirement that an insurance policy shall take any particular form, and, it appears, no legal need for the parties even to draw up a document. It is usual, though, for a distinctly formal document to be drawn up, in which are set out the terms of the insurers' obligations in return for the premiums to be paid. Further, the value of a written document emerges when disputes arise between insurers and assured. Often, the only way in which such disputes can be resolved is by interpreting the actual words used in the policy. For example, it may be vital to discover what

---

[1] See *Bufe* v. *Turner* (1815), 6 Taunt. 338.
[2] See *Condogianis* v. *Guardian Assurance Co., Ltd.*, [1921] 2 A.C. 125, P.C.

precisely is the peril against which insurance has been effected. Thus, suppose X has his house insured against the risk of fire and a fire breaks out which destroys his house, spreads to Y's premises, and, in so doing, causes damage which renders X legally liable to compensate Y. The problem then arises as to whether X's insurance covers him merely for the loss of his house, or whether it extends so as to cover also his responsibility to Y. The only satisfactory way in which such a problem could be resolved is by resorting to the policy and interpreting the relevant paragraphs. *LEGAL INTERPRIT*

(ii) *The peril of fire*

Having considered from various aspects the contract concluded between insurers and assured, the next matter which demands attention is the peril against which protection is sought. As its name implies, a fire insurance policy is designed to protect the assured in the event of his suffering a loss caused by fire, but exactly what legal significance is given to the idea of a loss "caused by fire?"

To begin with, let us concentrate purely on the "fire". When a policy of insurance speaks of fire, it means actual ignition, and moreover, what is ignited must not have been intended to ignite. The *cause* of the fire, though, other than in two instances, does not matter. What, then, are the two instances in which the cause of the fire does matter? The first is where the fire is deliberately caused by the assured with the intention of destroying the property insured. In such a case no claim can be made by him. Again, the second instance is where the fire is caused by what is known as an "excepted peril", for in that circumstance also no claim can be made under the policy. So what are meant by "excepted perils"? They are a series of causes of fire which are frequently listed in fire policies and for which no claim will be entertained by the insurers, i.e., they are "excepted". Included in such lists will be causes like war, riot and explosions.

Still in the same context, the next point to raise is whether the assured can claim under a policy only if his loss is occasioned by a fire which is *accidentally* begun. Here we find there is no such restriction. Very often fires are due to negligence, and it is to some extent the purpose of a policy of fire insurance to protect

71

the assured from careless acts or omissions.[3] Moreover, if loss is suffered by the assured on account of a fire which has a negligent origin, it does not matter whether the negligence is that of the assured, his servant or a stranger;[4] the assured can still make his claim.

Finally, on the matter of "fire", what of the innumerable fires which are deliberately lit, for instance, in ordinary domestic fireplaces? Often, property is accidentally destroyed by such fires. It is quite clear, though, that where loss is occasioned in this way, the assured will be protected by his policy.[5]

Now we must proceed to the idea of a loss being *caused* by fire, and try to distinguish between loss which is *directly caused* by fire, and loss which is only *remotely caused* by fire. By an ordinary policy of fire insurance the former is covered, but not the latter.

When a person makes a claim under a policy he does not have to show that the property which is the subject matter of the policy has in fact been burned. Fire can be the direct cause of a loss without actually burning the property involved. For example, a loss is directly caused by fire where property is damaged or destroyed in an effort to remove it from the path of the fire, or where property is so affected by water being used to extinguish the flames, or again where property in a burning building is so affected by the collapse of the structure. In all such instances, the property which is the subject of the policy may not be burned, but its damage or destruction, and hence the loss, is nevertheless directly caused by fire in the sense that but for the fire the property would still be intact.

In contrast, there is the loss which results only remotely from fire, and for which, as I said, no claim can be made. For example, the loss of business property which is destroyed by a fire can involve the owner in the further loss of business profits, and such loss of profits is considered merely a *consequential*, not a *direct* loss. It is noteworthy, however, that to cover losses of this variety it is possible to enter into special insurances.

---

[3]See for example, *A.-G.* v. *Adelaide S.S. Co.*, [1923] A.C. 292, H.L., at p. 308, *per* Lord WRENBURY.
[4]*Shaw* v. *Robberds* (1837), 6 Ad. & El. 75.
[5]*Harris* v. *Poland*, [1941] 1 All E.R. 204.

(iii) *Recovery under the policy*

In the event of the assured suffering a loss which is covered by his policy, the question arises as to how much money he is able to recover. The idea is that he must be fully "indemnified", by which we mean that he must be restored to the position which existed at the time of the fire. In other words, how much he can recover is measured *by the amount of the loss which he has suffered*. If the property is completely destroyed, then, in order to restore the assured to his former position (i.e., in order to indemnify him), he must be given the value of the property. If, on the other hand, the property is only partially destroyed, the loss can be generally made good by repairing the damage done. Accordingly, how much the assured can recover in that instance is measured by the cost of the repairs.

In the context of recovery, furthermore, a simple but vital matter must never be forgotten. It is a characteristic of a fire insurance policy that it always specifies the sum insured. This means that it speaks of a sum which is the *maximum* sum for which the insurers will accept liability. Thus, the insurers will indemnify the assured by paying him any sum *up to that amount but not above it*. If the measure of his loss is greater than the sum insured, NOTE then it follows that he cannot be completely indemnified. ← NOTE.

Sometimes, the fact that the policy specifies the sum insured causes confusion, and the view is erroneously taken that this is the amount which will be automatically recovered. Inasmuch as the whole idea is to restore the assured by making good his loss, it is clear that in order to recover the sum insured, he would have to prove a loss *of that amount*. By specifying the sum insured the insurers are really providing a ceiling, and saying in effect, "you can recover sums of money which represent losses up to and including the amount specified in the policy, but not beyond".

(iv) *"Reinstatement"*

Our final concern is with the idea of "reinstatement", by which is meant the physical restoration of property which has been damaged or destroyed by fire to its previous condition, and which, according to circumstances, can involve rebuilding, replacing, or repairing.

It may happen that the assured would prefer to be reinstated

73

than to receive a sum of money, or on the other hand, that the insurers would rather reinstate than make a payment. Equally, the converse could be true on either side, and the question remains, what is the position?

Under s. 83 of the Fires Prevention (Metropolis) Act 1774 (a statute which, as we have seen, applies despite its title, throughout England and Wales), the directors of any insurance company in which any house or building is insured against fire are required by statute, in case of loss or damage by fire, to reinstate it, upon the request of any person interested in it or entitled to it.

In fulfilling their obligations under this section the directors of the company cannot be compelled to spend more than the sum assured, and furthermore, if the directors do not receive a clear request[6] for reinstatement they can with impunity pay the insurance money to the assured.

In cases to which s. 83 does not extend, there is a fundamental obligation on the insurers to pay money, and, unless the assured is happy with the arrangement, they cannot substitute this obligation with an offer to reinstate. Generally, however, insurers overcome this fundamental obligation to pay money by expressly including in the policy an option to reinstate. Where such an option exists, it operates to the exclusive advantage of the insurers. They can please themselves which method they adopt, and the assured has no legal right to force them into pursuing either course.

CONCLUSION

While the nature and scope of this little book renders it appropriate only to have given a brief outline of the principles governing fire insurance, it is recommended that any persons who are particularly interested in this aspect of fire, read Professor Ivamy's book on *Fire and Motor Insurance*,[7] in which will be found a detailed and penetrating survey of fire insurance law.

The subject cannot be left, however, without reference to the significance of fire insurance in the realms of fire prevention.

---

[6]Persons who can so request include owners, mortgagors, mortgagees, lessors and lessees.
[7]Published by Butterworths.

Such are the powers of financial persuasion enjoyed by insurance companies that they could do much to remove the apathetic attitude which generally prevails in this country towards the problems of fire and fire prevention. Their influence ranges from one end of society to the other, and it is an influence which could be used both negatively to condemn indifference towards bad fire risks, and positively to promote interest in fire precautions.[8] In the narrow view, a contract of fire insurance is but a means of protection, and directly impinges only on the insurers and the assured; but in the wide view, it is a potential weapon in the battle of fire prevention, and so indirectly impinges on society at large.

[N.B. For those to whom Fire Insurance is of particular interest, a note is contained in Appendix II on a body known as the "London Salvage Corps".]

---

[8]See, in this connection, the report of the Departmental Committee on the Fire Service (Cmnd 4371), (Chapter 16, Insurance and the Fire Problem). In the last chapter of this book, considerable reference is made to this Report.

Chapter 6

THE FUTURE

Our concern in this, the final chapter, lies exclusively with the future. It is a fundamental characteristic of law that it never stands still, but grows and changes with the community which it serves, and the daily life of which it reflects. It is, perhaps, obvious, that the laws which meet the needs of one century will not satisfy the requirements of another, and nowhere is this shown more clearly than in the area of law concerned with fire. In the recent Fire Precautions Act we have an excellent example of legislation designed expressly to cope with the problems of a sophisticated, complex society. It is not only, though, in the arena of fire precautions that the wind of change has been blowing. Before long, it may well be that alterations are made in the legal structure of the fire service itself.

In May, 1970, there was presented to Parliament the report of the Departmental Committee on the Fire Service.[1] Under the chairmanship of Sir Ronald Holroyd, this committee was set up in February, 1967 to inquire into and make recommendations on matters including the principles which should govern the organisation of the fire service in Great Britain; the relationship between the central government and local fire authorities; and the functions of the fire service. The report runs to some two

---

[1]Cmnd 4371. [It is noteworthy that considerable attention was also paid to the need for further fire prevention measures.]

hundred pages in length, and reflects not only the extensive nature of the undertaking, but the industry with which members of the committee conducted their detailed inquiries, and the care with which they made their equally detailed recommendations. For our purpose, however, it will be sufficient if we confine ourselves to a survey of certain of their principal findings and recommendations:

(i) *The principles which should govern the organisation of the fire service*

As a result of their inquiries into the principles which should govern the organisation of the fire service, the members of the committee recommended that fire brigades should remain under local authority control, but found there was a strong case in terms of "operational efficiency" for "larger and more uniform fire authorities". From the evidence supplied, the conclusion was reached that "the future organisation of the fire service in England and Wales should be based upon a much smaller number of units than at present . . ." Thus, it was discovered by the committee that "the larger the area protected by one brigade, the greater the ability to plan fire cover and to mobilise and concentrate resources wherever they are needed . . ."; in other words, that larger and more uniform areas provide the advantage of more "rapid and effective mobilisation". The committee recognised, however, that the future of the fire service was but one aspect of the comprehensive review of local government contemporaneously being undertaken, and that the enactment of comprehensive legislation might take a long time. Further, the members of the committee thought it unlikely that separate legislation would be introduced to deal purely with the re-organisation of the fire service, but emphasised their view that "the regrouping of the fire service into larger units" was a vital and urgent matter.[2]

(ii) *The relationship between the central government and local fire authorities*

From their consideration of the principles which should govern

---

[2] The findings and recommendations of the committee in regard to the principles which should govern the organisation of the fire service can be found in Chapter 3 of the Report.

the organisation of the fire service, the members of the committee went on to conduct inquiries into the relationship between the central government and local fire authorities. On this aspect of the matter they found, *inter alia*, that there was "no existing organisation with specific responsibility for the collation of information for the study of basic fire problems, and for the provision of managerial services and guidance to the fire service". Such work, they thought, "should be undertaken centrally", and recommended that it be carried out by "an enlarged and strengthened Fire Department of the Home Office". In this connection they further recommended that the Secretary of State should be given "specific statutory responsibility for promoting the efficiency of the fire service and for providing research and management services". Again, so far as the Secretary of State's existing powers of control under the Fire Services Acts were concerned, the view was taken that these should be retained. Finally in this context it is important to note that in dealing with the relationship between the central government and local fire authorities, the members emphasised strongly that they had no desire and saw no need "to reduce the freedom of action of local fire authorities".[3]

(iii) *The functions of the fire service*

The Committee considered next the functions of the fire service, pointing out that those functions fall into three categories, viz: (a) the extinction of fires and the protection of life and property in case of fire; (b) fire prevention; and (c) special services (i.e., those covering a wide range of accidents and other major or minor emergency situations).

The functions mentioned in the first category derive, as the committee explained, from the statutory duties placed on fire authorities under the Fire Services Acts. (If one looks back to Chapter 2 one will recall that chief of those duties is the duty placed on fire authorities by s. 1 of the Fire Services Act 1947, to make provision for fire fighting purposes, and in particular to maintain a brigade of sufficient strength to meet all normal

---

[3]The findings and recommendations of the committee on the relationship between the central government and local fire authorities can be found in Chapter 4 of the Report.

requirements, to secure the efficient training of the brigade, to provide efficient arrangements for dealing with calls, to obtain information required for fire fighting purposes, to organise salvage operations, and to provide arrangements for giving advice on fire prevention.) The committee received no evidence to suggest that any difficulty arose from either this section or the other relevant statutory provisions, and accordingly recommended that no change should be made "in the existing statutory provisions from which the fire service derive their responsibility for extinguishing fires and protecting life and property in case of fire".

Postponing fire prevention as a topic for separate consideration, the committee then passed to a consideration of the third mentioned category of functions, namely, special services.

In dealing with this aspect of fire service functions, the committee explained that fire authorities are under no duty (other than in situations involving fire or the risk of fire) to provide a rescue service, but that under s. 3(1)(e) of the Fire Services Act 1947, they have a discretionary power to employ their brigades for purposes other than fire-fighting. It would be "an unnecessary and expansive burden", the committee felt, to place on fire authorities a statutory obligation to provide an emergency rescue service, and accordingly the recommendation was made that fire authorities "should continue to have statutory discretion to employ their brigades on . . . special service calls".

While considering special service calls, attention must be drawn also to a representation made to the committee with regard to the position of firemen who go out on such calls. It was pointed out that s. 30 of the Fire Services Act 1947 gives a fireman power to enter premises for fire-fighting purposes without the consent of the owner or occupier, but that there is no similar power in existence which would cover a fireman's actions on a special service call. The committee therefore recommended that firemen's powers of entry for fire-fighting purposes should be extended so as to cover special service calls.[4]

---

[4] The findings and recommendations of the committee on the functions of the fire service can be found in Chapter 5 of the Report. Note further that the committee devoted a short chapter exclusively to the future of industrial fire brigades, a matter which is dealt with in Appendix III.

At this juncture, mention must be made again of the fact that much consideration was given also to the need for further fire prevention measures, it being agreed by the members that while people could be induced to make provision for fire prevention through publicity and advice, and persuaded to do so through financial inducements,[5] in fact legislation was "one of the major weapons for attacking the fire problem".

In making recommendations for the reform of fire prevention legislation, the members believed to be an impracticable venture the suggestion that all such legislation should be consolidated into a single, comprehensive Fire Safety Act, but were greatly in agreement with the suggestion that "fire authorities should be responsible for enforcing all fire prevention legislation directed at premises when they have been occupied", for they were quick to recognise the difficulties arising when responsibility for enforcement resides with a variety of authorities.[6]

Inasmuch as the committee attached "the greatest importance" to any measures improving the effectiveness of fire prevention legislation, for instance "by widening its scope, by making the requirements of the various Acts as uniform as possible, and by seeing that its implementation is in the most suitable hands," the Fire Precautions Act must appear to the members as a step in the right direction. As it is gradually brought into operation, it will to a considerable extent achieve the type of improvement which they envisage.[7]

As might be expected in a chapter devoted to the future, the conclusion is on a speculative note. In particular, three questions

---

[5]Regarding financial inducements, it is interesting to note that the committee referred to the way in which the insurance industry has provided an economic incentive for fire prevention in industry and commerce, and recommended that insurance companies should give serious consideration to the possibility that they might have equal influence in the domestic sphere, by devising schemes which are based on the idea "of rewarding the conscientious and penalising the careless".

[6]For example, as the committee pointed out, under the Factories Act 1961 the fire authorities are normally responsible for granting means of escape certificates but provisions dealing with fire alarms and fire-fighting equipment fall within the province of H.M. Factory Inspectorate.

[7]Reference must be made once more to the fact that the Department of Employment and Productivity is in the midst of preparing a comprehensive revision of the Factories Act 1961, and the Offices, Shops and Railway Premises Act 1963, the object being to "widen the scope of the provisions, bring existing premises not at present covered within the ambit of a single, new Act", and place responsibility on the fire authorities for inspecting and certifying most of the premises involved.

appear to be raised. First, is one likely to see in the near future, "the regrouping of the fire service into larger units", a matter thought by the committee to be both vital and urgent? Again, will it be long before the Department of Employment and Productivity produces a bill revising the Factories Act and the Offices, Shops and Railway Premises Act? And last but by no means least, how many years will it take for the Fire Precautions Act to become fully operational?

In such affairs one cannot hazard a guess. All one can say is that the desire to effect legislative additions to or alterations in the law relating to fire is not a desire calculated to meet undue obstacles, for this is a sphere of law in which the aims of any legislation or delegated legislation introduced are clearly in the public interest, and carry their own inherent justification.[8] Indeed, one need seek no further for the precise nature of that justification than the fire service motto itself, which is, quite simply, "to save life". It is a motto which reflects faith in Him who gave life, hope for its preservation, and charity towards those who are in peril of its loss.

---

[8]Contrasts may be drawn with legislation and delegated legislation which impinges upon controversial issues of a social or an economic nature.

Appendix I

NOTE ON FIRE PRECAUTIONS IN THE CONTEXT OF CONSUMER PROTECTION

The object of the Consumer Protection Act 1961 is to ensure that goods which reach the members of the public do not in any way endanger their personal, physical safety. To achieve this object, the Act begins, in s. 1, by giving the Secretary of State power to make regulations imposing any such requirements as to the composition, contents, design, construction, finish or packing of such goods as he prescribes, and as to the warnings or instructions to be sent with such goods, as are, in his opinion expedient to prevent or reduce the risk of death or personal injury. Section 2 then continues the attack by prohibiting the selling of goods which do not comply with any regulations which the Secretary of State should make, although it must be noted that the section contains a list of exceptions from the prohibition, including, for example, the selling of goods as "scrap", and the selling of goods which it is reasonably believed arc not to he used in Great Britain.

For the seller who attempts to sell goods which do not comply with any regulations made by the Secretary, two distinct dangers lurk.[1] The Act not only makes it a criminal offence to sell such goods,[2] but also enables any purchaser affected by a sale to bring a civil action against the vendor.

---

[1] See s. 3 of the Act.
[2] It is a defence for the seller to show that he had reasonable cause to believe that all the requirements were satisfied (see s. 3(2)).

Even then we must proceed further, for the Act gives local authorities power to inspect goods, and to purchase goods for the purpose of testing them.

Passing on from the provisions of the Act to the regulations which have been made thereunder by the Secretary of State, we must consider:

(i) *The Oil Heaters Regulations* 1962 *and* 1966

The Oil Heaters Regulations 1962[3] (as amended by the Oil Heaters Regulations 1966)[4], contain detailed and stringent requirements regarding the construction and design of oil heaters. The numerous matters upon which they impinge include stability, draught resistance, fuel temperature, and standard of performance. Again, great importance is attached to the acquaintance of the purchaser with the dangers inherent in his purchase. Thus the regulations require oil heaters to bear legible and durable warnings against the use of petrol as a fuel, against carriage when alight, and against use in places where they might be knocked over, or places which are draughty or unventilated.

(ii) *The Nightdresses (Safety) Regulations* 1967

The Nightdresses (Safety) Regulations[5] make a distinction between nightdresses designed for children and those designed for adults. There is a strict requirement that (*inter alia*) the fabric used in the making of children's nightdresses be of a kind capable of satisfying the requirements of the British Standard for fabrics "described as of low flammability". With regard to adults' nightdresses, however, it is sufficient if either the fabric of which they are made complies with the above requirement, or else they carry durable warnings that they must be kept away from fire. Furthermore, the regulations impose the requirement that nightdresses the fabric of which is chemically treated so as to increase its safety, shall bear a durable warning against the advisability of certain cleansing operations.

---

[3]S.I. 1962 No. 884.
[4]S.I. 1966 No. 588.
[5]S.I. 1967 No. 839.

(iii) *The Toys (Safety) Regulations* 1967

From the fire precautions point of view, the Toys (Safety) Regulations[6] are of interest inasmuch as they prohibit the use of celluloid in toys other than "ping-pong" balls.

---

[6]S.I. 1967 No. 1157.

Appendix II

NOTE ON THE LONDON SALVAGE CORPS

The London Salvage Corps is a force of men established and maintained by insurance companies to protect the interests of those companies by attending fires and taking steps to minimise the loss occasioned to the premises involved.[1] Obviously, the activities of the Corps extend over a wide range, but chief amongst them are the following:

(a) Removing smoke and water from premises, and preventing the spreading of water.

(b) Covering damaged premises with tarpaulins.

(c) Moving the contents of premises, and covering the contents with tarpaulins.

(d) Taking steps to prevent stock from deteriorating.

(e) Drying and cleaning machinery.

(f) Keeping a watch on the premises in case fire should break out again or in case any theft should be attempted.

Further, under s. 29 of the Metropolitan Fire Brigade Act 1865, the fire brigade is obliged to render necessary assistance to the members of the force in the performance of their duties,

---

[1]For details as to the financing of the Corps (the way in which charges are apportioned between the insurers and so on), see Doublet, *Fire Insurance Claims, Law and Practice*, 1963, p. 186 (Pitman). (Note also that the Corps turn out, *as a public service*, to certain properties, such as Royal Palaces.)

and obliged, upon the application of any officer of the force, to hand over to their custody any property which may be saved from fire. Moreover, no charge can be made for the services rendered by the fire brigade in this sphere.[2]

---

[2]It is worthy of note that under s. 13, Metropolitan Fire Brigade Act 1865, as amended by s. 48(3), London Government Act 1963, every insurance company insuring from fire any property in Greater London is required to make an annual contribution to the expenses of the London fire brigade.

Appendix III

NOTE ON THE FUTURE OF INDUSTRIAL FIRE BRIGADES

Some readers may be interested to note that in the report of the Departmental Committee on the Fire Service[1] there is a short chapter devoted exclusively to the future of fire brigades privately maintained by certain industrial establishments . . .[2]

Facts found

A number of industrial establishments, the committee found, maintain full-time or part-time works fire brigades. Such brigades vary considerably in size and quality, and, inasmuch as they rest purely on voluntary action, are subject to no statutory control. Again, the present trend as regards private cover of this nature (and a trend which the committee expected to continue), is for more industrial establishments to leave actual fire fighting in the hands of the local authority fire brigades, and "to concentrate their private efforts on fire prevention measures". In spite of this *general* trend, however, the committee emphasised that certain establishments would wish nevertheless to continue the provision of private works brigades: establishments such as, for instance, "high risk" industrial installations erected in

---

[1]Cmnd. 4371.
[2]See Chapter 6 of the Report.

7

relatively remote areas, and industrial organisations with complicated high risk processes.

Suggestions received, conclusions and recommendations

During the course of the investigations conducted into the
functioning of industrial fire brigades, the members of the committee received suggestions that mandatory requirements should
be imposed upon works brigades. Thus, it was suggested that
industrial brigades should be "affiliated to local authority brigades and become subject to approved standards of efficiency",
or, alternatively, that local authority brigades should have a
"mandatory duty to inspect industrial brigades and approve
their efficiency, organisation and equipment".

The members of the committee came to the conclusion,
though, that to impose mandatory requirements on industrial
concerns which voluntary provide works brigades was "unde-
sirable and unnecessary". Evidence was given of excellent
co-operation between works and local authority brigades, and the
committee felt that where there was such a genuine willingness
to co-operate much could be done without mandatory requirements.

Again, attention must be drawn to the point that the "availability of a works fire brigade in no way alters the responsibility
of the local authority fire brigade to attend a fire if called".
With regard to calling for the help of the local authority brigade
the committee recommended that the industrial management and
the chief officer of the local authority brigade should discuss the
circumstances in which the brigade should be called, and that
the management should impress on the works brigades the
importance of erring on the safe side when considering whether
to call for outside help. Indeed, fire authorities and industrial
concerns often arrange by agreement (and usually it is a very
precisely drawn agreement) that the private brigade will attend
incidents which occur outside the boundaries of their own
premises. Such arrangments are not, of course, without their
possible legal problems. Take, for instance, the question of the
indemnification of the fire authority against loss or damage
arising due to the negligence of the "private" fireman while
acting on behalf of the fire authority. (Often, a good plan is for

the "private" fireman to become a part-time volunteer member of the fire authority's fire brigade, if he can be persuaded so to do.) The committee did not feel that an obligation should be imposed on a works fire brigade to notify the local authority brigade immediately a fire breaks out.

To sum up

The recommendations made, therefore, were of a relatively minor character: no major recommendation was made to bring industrial fire brigades under any form of statutory control. From the state of affairs which the members of the committee found to exist, they were clearly satisfied that these brigades are able to meet efficiently the need which they are designed to fulfil.

Appendix IV

NOTE ON LEGISLATION AND DELEGATED LEGISLATION

In both Chapters 2 and 3 we are concerned with legislation, and (to a lesser extent), with delegated legislation, so it may prove helpful to say a little more about each.

It will be recalled that legislation is law made in a formal fashion, and that, inasmuch as it emanates from the Sovereign, it is regarded as the most important source of law. What, though, does it look like? What is to be found if one glances through an Act of Parliament?

To begin with, there will be what is called the short title of the Act, i.e., a name for easy reference[1] (for example, the Fire Services Act 1947). Straight after that, though, one finds the long title of the Act. This begins "An Act to . . .", and the words which follow describe briefly the particular purposes of the Act. So, if one looks at the Fire Services Act 1947, one finds at the beginning a rather long paragraph which commences, "An Act to make further provision for fire services in Great Britain . . ." and continues with a number of objects in that sphere.

After the long title one comes to the "words of enactment", i.e., the words which indicate that certain rules *are being made*. These read:

"Be it enacted by the Queen's most Excellent Majesty, by and

---

[1]One would stress the word *easy*, for there is also a technical method by which reference may be made to an Act of Parliament.

with the advice and consent of the Lords Spiritual and Temporal, and Commons, in this present Parliament assembled, and by the authority of the same, as follows:"

Then one arrives at the heart of the matter: one comes to the actual rules which are being laid down.

The rules which are being laid down are arranged in numbered sections, and, if it is a long Act of Parliament, the sections are put into groups. Moreover, at the top of each group there is a brief heading, telling the reader about the subject matter of the particular group of sections. So, if one looks again in the Fire Services Act 1947, one will find such headings as "Fire Authorities" and "Supply of Water for Fire Fighting", and underneath each a number of sections set out. Further, to help clarify matters still more, there is in very small print at the side of each section a brief note of the content of that section.

Now let us consider in more detail the actual "section". Each section may contain a number[2] of separate and distinct points, and so that they can be clearly set out the section is often divided into "subsections". Like the sections themselves, each subsection is numbered, but the number is put in brackets. So, to take a couple of random examples, one is likely to find in an Act a Section 1, subsection (2), a section 4, subsection (3), . . . and so on. (In text books it is usually to be found written as s. 1(2), s. 4(3) . . . and so on).[3]

If, as is often the case, it is necessary to make *further* subdivisions, they are referred to as "paragraphs" and "subparagraphs". So, for instance, if one looks yet once more at the Fire Services Act 1947 and considers the first section, one will find there is section 1, subsection (1), paragraphs (*a*) to (*f*). Again, in a text book, a reference to one of those paragraphs would appear as s. 1(1)(*a*), s. 1(1)(*b*), . . . and so on.

At the very end of an Act of Parliament (but just as much a part of the Act as the sections), one may find what are known as "Schedules". The idea is this: to make things clear, the subject matter of the Act is divided between sections and Schedules. In the sections appear the principles and an introduction to the schedules, while in the Schedules appear the small details.

---

[2] Indeed, *any* number.
[3] The reader will usually find it written that way in this book.

APPENDIX IV

At first sight, the "lay-out" of an Act of Parliament may seem strange, but, as the reader becomes used to it, he will realise that the pattern is one which is designed to promote clarity and certainty.

Now we must turn from legislation to delegated legislation, and here a somewhat shorter note will suffice, for delegated legislation will not occupy so much of our time.

Delegated legislation, as has been explained, is legislation which is made by certain persons and bodies who are empowered by Parliament so to act. It is essentially a "time saving" device. Furthermore, it is important to bear in mind that while such legislation has the force of an ordinary Act of Parliament, there is a big difference between the two, viz: *The validity of delegated legislation can be challenged in the courts, but this is not so with ordinary legislation; it is not open to challenge in that way.*

In this country there is no shortage of delegated legislation, on the contrary, there is an excess of it, and it emerges from numerous sources. Thus, to take some examples, there are statutory Orders in Council made by the Queen in Council,[4] ministerial and departmental regulations issued by Ministers and heads of government departments,[5] and bye-laws made by local authorities and by Public Corporations. Unfortunately, though, the whole field of delegated legislation is in an untidy state, because, *inter alia*, the terms used are not used with any precision. For instance, the delegated legislation produced by Ministers emerges as "rules", "regulations", "schemes", "orders", "directions" and so forth; all these labels being used indiscriminately. So far as we are concerned, however, it may help if it is pointed out that the delegated legislation which we shall meet is of the more important kind, and the documents in which it appears are known as "statutory instruments".[6] Further, when one comes to read these statutory instruments,[7] it will be found that the rules which they contain are set out in a pattern similar to that used in an ordinary Act of Parliament.

---

[4]These are a very grand and dignified sort of delegated legislation.
[5]These also are regarded as delegated legislation of the more important variety.
[6]Even so, care should be taken to remember that not any and every piece of delegated legislation is made by statutory instrument.
[7]They may appear as "orders" or "regulations"—it is useful always to remember the labels are used indiscriminately.

ADDENDA

After this little book went to press, significant events occurred concerning the Fire Precautions Act, and attention is now drawn to them:—

(1) If the reader looks back to p.50 he will be reminded that s.44(3) of the Act provides for the Act to come into operation on such day as the Secretary of State may appoint, and further provides that different dates may be appointed for different purposes. On February 21st, 1972 an order was made entitled the 'Fire Precautions Act 1971 (Commencement No. 1) Order 1972,' which brought into operation on March 20th, 1972 *the greater part* of the Fire Precautions Act. It should be noticed that, of the sections of the Act to which reference has been made, ss.3, 4 and 12 (and part of s.19), have not yet been brought into force.

(2) If the reader looks back to pp. 50-51 he will recollect that s.1 of the Act provides that a fire certificate shall be compulsory for premises which are put to certain uses, and enables the Secretary of State to "designate" uses for that purpose. By virtue of the Order referred to in paragraph 1 above, s.1 came into operation on March 20th, 1972, and straight away the power to designate has been put into action. By an Order entitled the 'Fire Precautions (Hotels and Boarding Houses) Order 1972', the Secretary of State has designated, (for the purpose of requiring a fire certificate), the use of premises for a hotel or boarding house if sleeping accommodation is provided there for more than six persons (be those persons staff or guests), or there is sleeping accommodation above first-floor or below ground-floor level. It is important to notice, however, that this Order does not come into operation until June 1st, 1972.

(3) By regulations entitled the 'Fire Precautions (Application for Certificate) Regulations 1972', which came into operation on March 20th, 1972, there was prescribed a form of application for a fire certificate under the Fire Precautions Act. The form is set out in full in a Schedule to the regulations, and makes clear to the applicant the details required.

(4) In connection with the operation of the Fire Precautions

Act, there is being issued a "Guide to Fire Precautions in Hotels and Boarding Houses." In no way possessed of statutory force, its object is to provide guidance for both fire authorities and those responsible for the management of hotels and boarding houses. In the pursuit of that object, there are set out in the guide fundamental requirements concerning means of escape, means of giving warning in case of fire, fire fighting equipment, and fire instruction and drills. Moreover, the hope is evinced that the existence of such a guide may help to achieve throughout the country a uniform implementation of the Act to the relevant premises.

INDEX